Carceral World, Communal City

By

David H. Lukenbill

A Chulu Press Book

First Chulu Press Edition published
October 2008

ISBN-10: 0-9791670-5-1
ISBN-13: 978-0-9791670-5-8
PRINTED IN THE UNITED STATES OF AMERICA
First Edition

Published by The Lampstand Foundation

www.lampstandfoundation.org

For Marlene & Erika Always

Contents

Preface

If we do not embrace our past, we have no future.

1) $\mathfrak{I}$ open this book as I opened my first: Lukenbill (2006), to those criminals for whom it is written:

> [To] those who commit crimes for money, for whom crime is a way of life, and to whom the criminal world is a world with a subtly defined code of behavior and strong cultural connection.

I am not speaking in this book of those of whom Christ has spoken:

> 5. And he that shall receive one such child in my name, receiveth me.
> 6. But he that shall scandalize one of these little ones that believe in me, it were better for him that a mill-stone were hanged about his neck, and that he were drowned in the depth of the sea.
> 7. Wo to the world because of scandals. For it must needs be that scandals come: but, nevertheless wo to that man by whom the scandal cometh. (Matthew 18: 5-7, Douay Rheims)

And the explanatory notes from the University of Navarre (1988):

The holy, pained indignation sounding in Jesus' words show the seriousness of the sin of scandal, which is defined as something said, done or omitted which leads another person to commit sin" (*St Pius X Catechism, 417*)

"Millstone": our Lord is referring to a form of punishment used in ancient times which consisted in throwing a person into the sea with a heavy weight attached to his neck to prevent his body floating to the surface; this was regarded as a particularly ignominious form of death because it was inflicted only on the worst criminals and also because it meant deprival of burial.

Although Jesus affirms that people will cause others to sin, this does not mean that everyone, personally, should not ensure that this does not happen. Therefore, everyone who does cause another to sin is responsible for his action. Here he refers directly to scandal given to children—an action that is particularly malicious given the weakness and innocence of children. (p. 162)

The criminals of whom I speak are great sinners as was I, but like the prodigal son, are capable of transformation and may deserve our forgiveness if truly redeemed.

(*The Criminals Search for God,* E-Book Edition, pp. 6-8)

2) For the criminal to transform himself, he must accept, as penance for his criminal life, to live the rest of his life following the path of the saints; for this is the call to the apostolate, this is the call to the spiritual life; this is the path to atonement and forgiveness.

Maritain (1960) clarifies the ultimate call of the spiritual life:

> Dominating the whole spiritual life is the call to perfection.
>
> "Be you therefore perfect, as also your heavenly Father is perfect."
>
> "Christian perfection consists essentially in charity," says Saint Thomas. "Indeed a thing is said to be perfect in so far as it attains its proper end—the proper end of a thing being its ultimate perfection. Now it is charity that unites us to God, Who is the last end of the human soul: he that abideth in charity, abideth in God, and God in him." (p. 40)

3) This work is not about a theory of criminology, of which there are already many, nor a history of rehabilitation or of the prison, also many. My work looks at the terrain where crime, history, human and organizational behavior, and Catholicism walk along paths—through the criminal city—we cannot readily perceive, but within which I see a deep rubric of transformation, redemption, the prodigal son, and urban contemplative spiritual warriors, enriched by Catholic teaching.

This is not a book that will be embraced by many in the criminal justice field as it goes against the prevailing narrative, yet for those for whom it is written—penitential criminals—it may find a home.

4) For many years during its founding period, the study of criminology concerned itself with ultimate questions: What makes a criminal? Why do they do what they do? What kind of people are they? How do they change?

These questions occupied many of the founding criminologists, but for the past few decades criminology, with too few exceptions, seems to have turned its back on this and has become preoccupied with technical questions very narrow in scope and of little relevance to the criminal's life of crime or his rehabilitation.

The full prisons resulting from broken windows policing and three strikes sentencing reduced crime, but an unintended consequence is the growing influence of the criminal world—as it is more deeply shaped by the carceral—and a deepening corrosiveness of already crimogenic neighborhoods by the huge increase of reentering criminals.

Those reentering society have not been rehabilitated while in prison, nor do they have access or inclination to effective rehabilitative programs on the outside. Current research shows very few even exist and many actually make the problem worse. Consequently, they soon return to prison at a rate of around 70% nationally, of the 650,000 to 700,000 being released annually.

5) My work suggests a policy option of looking first to the 30% of reentering criminals who have succeeded, and from them seek out leaders who have gone on to higher education and have an inclination to become involved in developing and managing reentry programs; provide them with core funding, advanced Catholic social teaching training (which by definition includes ongoing catechetical education), and allow them to begin addressing this significant social problem from the deep knowledge of their own experience, education, and training.

6) The proper role of the state is to secure justice and the proper role of the Catholic Church is to encourage that just role of the state.

A cornerstone of justice, and the ultimate expression of the principle of subsidiarity, is to allow individuals to help themselves, to not impede their desire to do that.

For the state—primarily concerned with the increased level of public safety emanating from reformed criminals—it becomes a proper role of the Catholic Church to teach the state concerning the effective method of doing so. She does this through her teaching authority and through supporting apostolate work addressing criminal transformation.

7) To love those whom we fear and hate, those who have harmed us—as Pope John Paul II taught us so dramatically through his embracing and forgiving of the assassin in his cell—is a great teaching and is the great law personified for us who would breathe with the Church.

Yes, we must continue to lock up the criminal, we must continue to protect the innocent by holding fast to the criminal, embracing him in the carceral world which can become for him a pathway to redemption, as the necessary suffering imbues his every cellular hour, as it surely does.

8) The criminal world in the United States, with the carceral shaping of it, has become a coherent entity and within that entity it is the criminal world leadership to whom we must look for transformative leadership who have already transformed the pain of their suffering into the power of teaching others.

9) The history of the reformed criminal's involvement in defining and shaping transformation in the United States over the past several decades has moved from the glamorization of the revolutionary 1960's and 1970's which Gottschalk, (2006) describes as:

> Some members of the New Left became obsessed with the place of the prison in larger political struggles, according to Cummins. [1994: p. 125 & 127] The New Left began to idealize prisoners and started "thinking convicts, all convicts, were their soul-mates and could be their leaders." [Cummins, p. 128] Cummins contends that the radical left was guilty of uncritical crime fetishism as it embraced the "deviant convict hero," seeing him as a new model for the revolution.   [Cummins, p. 94]. (p. 180)

During the 1980's and 1990's, through the power of the crime victim's movement and the utilitarian success of such strategies as broken windows policing and three strikes sentencing, the involvement of the reformed criminal in rehabilitation work dropped considerably.

10) The emergence of the faith-based paradigm in social service work has helped bring former criminals back into the work, as has the contributions of reformed criminal scholars noted by Ross & Richards (2003):

> The emerging field of convict criminology consists primarily of essays and empirical research conducted and written by convicts or exconvicts, on their way to completing or already in possession of a Ph.D., or by enlightened academics who critique existing literature, policies and practices, thus contributing to a new perspective on criminology, criminal justice, corrections, and community corrections. (p. 6)

The continued involvement of criminals is also called for by Samara (n.d.):

> I reiterate my overall objective, which is to present the voices of activists and prisoners in an attempt to convince academics that the information and analysis they provide is crucial to the project of keeping criminology relevant. All good intentions and impeccable methods aside, without the insights of

people subjected to the reality of prisons in America the scholarship on crime and punishment will remain incomplete. Without grounding our work in the actuality of crime and punishment we cannot realistically hope to capture their complexities or their true implications for the social world. Only with this type of transformation of the criminological project can we hope to be relevant, critical and accurate. (#98)

It is this ground which I hope to further strengthen through this work, which is animated by the social teaching and my conversion to Catholicism.

11) We know from the very beginning of the Catholic Church what would be the reception of those who have fallen far and been redeemed as noted by Marks (2007):

> If Christ could befriend a former prostitute to the point of immortalizing her and appearing to her in his risen form before showing himself to any of his apostles, then the quality of divine mercy that led Our Lord to open paradise to the good thief is well in sight. (p.15)

Criminal justice throughout the history of the Kingdom of God, has been a balance between retribution and restoration, and though the pagans used death propitiously, the People of God valued human life of priceless coin, even the life of a criminal, as one, St. Dismas, the Good Thief, became the first canonized saint of the Church founded on Peter, and another, St. Callistus, becoming Peter.

Introduction
Transformative Teaching

We need deep knowledge leaders with the endurance and strength of spirit surviving the prison yard and the death row cell.

A Symbiotic Relationship

12) **T**he effectiveness of the criminal transformative teaching I am asserting is dependent upon the existence of a deep understanding of the principles of Catholic social teaching.

When I first began working with the social teaching and realized that the guiding principles animating it also formed the foundational ideas of the nonprofit sector, I assumed that the social teaching could be used effectively by anyone.

I now realize that—though that hope remains attainable—the most optimal use of the teaching can only come from being an active, well-catechized Catholic.

However, Merkle (2004) also instructs us on how to advance the knowledge of the social teaching of the Church in the world:

> Some ecologists say it is not the general conditions of an ecosystem that ultimately determine its capacity to sustain itself, but that single factor that is in short supply in a given system that determines its carrying capacity. Is community that single factor

that marks the Church's capacity to transform Social Catholicism for this new century? Some caution that the Church must link the social encyclical tradition to **new social carriers**, or face irrelevance in the social realm. These carriers might occupy different places along the sociological matrix of community: from association, to movements, or groups, yet as collectives within the Church, all have a common dimension in some degree. (p. 241, highlighting added)

13) Through the work of The Lampstand Foundation we plan to build a new platform from which the social teaching can enter into congruence with one of the "new social carriers" called for, and become part of the criminal transformative community.

Criminal transformation and Catholic social teaching form a symbiotic relationship, a natural law of criminal transformation, where the truth of the teaching is the only reality strong enough to trump the truth of the world—the city of men—which is the truth the criminal lives by.

14) Since the Enlightenment—the true Dark Ages—when the spiritual basis of worldly living was largely stripped from human societies, the life values of the world have reverted to those of pagan times, seasoned with modern technology's ability to glamorize, beautify, endow with meaning, and globalize.

It is impossible for agents of the world, though acting with the best of intentions and armed with sterling academic credentials and advanced professional certification, to transform criminals who live—in a clearer and more direct way than they—the values they live by rather than the ones they profess.

In the criminal world—particularly in prison—a central truth is that you have to walk the talk, you have to live your *proclaimed* truth for it to be accepted by others.

This is a profound concept deeply embedded in Catholic social teaching and the Church has walked her talk for two thousand years.

15) The unbroken line of truth spoken by the popes, fathers, doctors, and saints of the Church, is striking in its congruence to the truths proclaimed by its founder, Jesus Christ, and written down in the Gospels to teach us still.

No organization walks the talk as does the Catholic Church.

Social teaching is the talk of the Church and her saints are the walk.

16) The natural law is hard-wired into every human being by God—conscience and reason its guiding principles—and the social teaching is an expression of this law as it relates to how we are to live together.

As the Holy See (1997) teaches us:

> The soul only enters freely into the communion of love. God immediately touches and directly moves the heart of man. He has placed in man a longing for truth and goodness that only he can satisfy. (#2002)

17) A seminal thinker on criminal justice, Wilson (1983), speaking of rehabilitation wrote:

> It requires not merely optimistic but heroic assumptions about the nature of man to lead one to suppose that a person, finally sentenced after (in most cases) many brushes with the law, and having devoted a good part of his youth and young adulthood to misbehavior of every sort, should, by either the solemnity of prison or the skillfulness of a counselor, come to see the error of his ways and to experience a transformation of his character. (p. 163)

18) Having personally experienced both the "solemnity of prison [and] the skillfulness of a counselor" which were to no avail in changing my criminality—and knowing hundreds of other criminals with the same experience—it is true, neither generally results in transformation.

What does result in transformation, and what has always been the strongest influence on human beings one to another, is the wise counsel of a friend, a respected transformed criminal who has been where you have been and where you secretly want to go—the path of peace, harmony, and truth—man's ultimate dream and the search for which he is hard wired to continue to pursue once that of the city of men withers and dies.

This is a path discovered by untold millions throughout history within the embrace of the Church and through the vision embodied in the social teaching, delivered by a transformed criminal and a deep knowledge leader, so will criminals discover it.

Part One: Catholic Criminal Justice

Crime is essentially a theological problem and it is only within theology that evil—the deepest dimension of crime—can be addressed. It is evil which must concern us in addressing crime, and we must recognize that evil rarely reforms, but most criminals can, and will; given a reason and shown the way.

The Beginning

19) The first crime was Cain's slaying of Abel and the first murderer was punished by banishment—used as long as there were faraway places but with a planet digitally one world, prison is banishment—with a mark so no one would harm him and Cain became a builder of cities where crime grew, even through the deluge its sprit clung to earth.

The entire murderous sequence lays the ground for what has followed in the criminal world since:

> 1: Now Adam knew Eve his wife; and she conceived and bore Cain, saying: "I have gotten a man with the help of the Lord."
> 2: And again she bore his brother Abel. Now Abel was a keeper of sheep, and Cain a tiller of ground.
> 3: In the course of time Cain brought to the Lord an offering of the fruits of the ground,

4: and Abel brought of the firstlings of his flock and of their fat portions: and the Lord had regard for Abel and his offerings,

5: but for Cain and his offerings he had no regard. So Cain was very angry, and his countenance fell.

6: The Lord said to him: Why are you angry, and why has your countenance fallen?

7: If you do well, will you not be accepted? And if you do not do well, sin is crouching at the door; its desire is for you, but you must master it.

8: Cain said to Abel his brother, "Let us go out to the field." And when they were in the field, Cain rose up against his brother Abel, and killed him.

9: Then the Lord said to Cain: Where is Abel your brother?" He said, "I do not know; am I my brother's keeper?"

10: And the Lord said, "What have you done? The voice of your brother's blood is crying to me from the ground.

11: And now you are cursed from the ground which has opened its mouth to receive your brother's blood from your hand.

12: When you till the ground, it shall no longer yield to you its strength; you shall be a fugitive and wanderer on the earth,"

13: Cain said to the Lord, "My punishment is greater than I can bear.

14: Behold, thou hast driven me this day from the ground: and from thy face I shall be hidden: and I shall be a fugitive and a wanderer on the earth and whoever finds me will slay me."

15: Then the Lord said to him" Not so! If any one slays Cain, vengeance shall be taken on him sevenfold." And the Lord put a mark on Cain, lest any who came upon him should kill him.

16: Then Cain went away from the presence of the Lord, and dwelt in the land of Nod, east of Eden.

17: Cain knew his wife, and she conceived and bore Enoch; and he built a city, and called the name of the city after the name of his son, Enoch.

(Genesis 4: 1-17)

We see the anger and envy that desires the others death, the acceptance doing well generates, the separation from God sin creates, and the curse sin lays upon man's life even to the ground upon which he walks, the mark of protection that a life may not be taken for a life—perhaps a teaching on the death penalty—the criminal as eternal fugitive and wanderer, and the building of the city of men, the criminal city, home to the criminal world since.

Cain, in his greed would not share the first fruits of his work, and Abel, in his generosity shared the first fruits readily. Cain did not know that the spirit of the gift was more important than the flesh of it.

20) The first expression of the criminal law that became the fullness of the Church, embracing all Jews and Gentiles entering the Kingdom of God, is found in Exodus 20:22 to 23:33, the *Book of the Covenant.*

It details how to treat slaves, stating many violations calling for death: striking another that he dies, striking your father or mother, stealing a man.

It outlaws charging the poor interest on money loaned to them, calls for resting on the seventh day, and instructs not to oppress the stranger.

21) The Pontifical Council for Justice and Peace (2004) noted:

> Every sin is *personal* under a certain aspect; under another, every sin is *social* insofar as and because it also has social consequences.... (#117, italics in original)

> *Certain sins, moreover, constitute by their very object a direct assault on one's neighbor. Such sins in particular are known as social sins.* Social sin is every sin committed against the justice due in relations between individuals, between the individual and the community, and also between the community and the individual. (#118, italics in original)

Every criminal act is personal, from a person it comes, from an idea shaping action, from desire and want, and as it moves from the person into the world, assaulting our neighbor—whom we have been instructed to love—it becomes crime against the justice balanced between individuals and the world, the justice we all have an inalienable right to expect, the dignity each of us deserves from each other.

22) Skotnicki (2004) notes foundational ideas of Catholic criminal justice:

> There has been a hard-won synthesis in the development of the three foundations of Catholic thought on criminal justice; they form, in effect, a continuum proceeding from the warrant to punish, to the place and program of both penance and reform, and culminating in the ritual of return and reinstatement. One cannot limit the value of one of the three elements without significantly altering the meaning of the other two. (p. 812)

23) The Decalogue defines the wrong requiring punishment, prison time is the penitential place and program, and reentry— though still being sought in its new manifestations of success, one can see the Rite of Christian Initiation for Adults (RCIA) as a model—the ritual path to communal reentry.

Pope John Paul II (2000) has spoken to us of punishment:

> Punishment and imprisonment have meaning if, while maintaining the demands of justice and discouraging crime, *they serve the rehabilitation of the individual* by offering those who have made a mistake an opportunity to reflect and to change their

lives in order to be fully reintegrated into society. (#6 italics in original)

24) Many criminal justice scholars, who are attempting to come to terms with their own fear and trepidation about prison, see it as a central animating concept to modern life; and prison's punishing reality, where the most intimate violations and terror clouding men's minds is thus objectified, shaped, and placed within comfortable theories and explanatory ideologies.

25) For the Catholic perspective on criminal justice, the animating factor is justice. Seeing prison as the shaper of criminal world values, the central animating factor of Catholic criminal justice is the human being, the redeemable human being, shorn of his terror-creating presence and humble in the sight of God, a quiet neighbor to men.

26) We see how the classic expressions of justice from Catholic social teaching and tradition inform different aspects of the criminal path—distributive (fair social distribution of resources, the criminal feels it is his right to steal)—commutative (to each his own)—with the prison as penitential (justice for crime, do the crime, do the time), yet the criminal will rarely consider transformation, and transformative justice (seeing distance from God, spiritual interiority, the relation with our creator as root cause, as the city of men defines the truth as he lives it) and he must learn or, more correctly, be taught the eternal truth which will lead him out of the criminal city.

27) In the history of the saints of the Church we see great transformative stories.

We know the first criminal to become a saint was Dismas, the Good Thief, crucified alongside of Christ who Christ took with him from Calvary to heaven.

The first criminal to become a Pope and later saint, was Callistus I who died a martyr but was Pope for five years, from 217 to 222.

The first Catholic criminologist was surely St. Augustine, who in his developed reasoning around the city of men in his masterpiece, *The City of God*, essentially lays out the world whose truth criminals embrace in their descent into the criminal world.

28) It is fitting that the United States is a country where Catholic Criminal Justice might form strong roots—for though the term has possibly been used elsewhere, it is most congruent here, in America, where the prison world has grown in ways rarely imagined

The United States, even before it was the United States was a Catholic land, as Archbishop Gomez notes: (2007):

> As you well know, your Catholic and Hispanic roots here in Arizona go even deeper. It is amazing to think that the Gospel was preached to the indigenous peoples here in the 1530's, by missionaries sent from Mexico...*long before the United States of America was even an idea, this land was Catholic.*
>
> Every American today, in some way traces his or her roots to the great Hispanic-

Catholic missions of the 16th and 17th centuries. We feel this deeply here in the Southwest. In other parts of our country, Americans proudly trace their roots more deeply to the early Catholic missions of immigrants from other foreign lands, France, Poland, Germany, Ireland and Italy. (p. 3-4)

29) In California, the locus of the American prison system and its most defining metaphor, the first civil governor was a devout convert to Catholicism, the lawyer Peter H. Burnett, who constructed a book of his conversion, built upon the legal reasoning of a massive brief comprising 800 plus pages and holding such sway in its power that it has been described by one reviewer as "how the romance of Rome could transform the romance of the old West." (Joseph Pierce in Burnett, (2004) end page)

30) Then, the concepts animating Catholic Criminal Justice are:

a) Justice, according to the Holy See (1997):

> The cardinal moral virtue which consists in the constant and firm will to give their due to God and to neighbor. *Original* justice refers to the state of holiness in which God created our first parents.
> *Commutative* justice, which obliges respect for the rights of the other, is required by the seventh commandment; it is distinguished from *legal* justice, which concerns what the

citizen owes to the community, and *distributive* justice, which regulates what the community owes its citizens in proportion to their contributions and needs. (p. 895)

Social Justice: The respect for the human person and the rights which flow from human dignity and guarantee it. Society must provide the conditions that allow people to obtain what is their due, according to their nature and vocation. (p. 899)

31) This understanding of justice and its different aspects embraces the entire range of idea and polices that under gird Catholic Criminal Justice.

b) Crime is sin and sin is:

An offense against God as well as a fault against reason, truth, and right conscience. Sin is a deliberate thought, word, deed or omission contrary to the eternal law of God. In judging the gravity of sin, it is customary to distinguish between mortal and venial sins. (Holy See, 1997, p.899)

c) The sins of the criminal are mortal sins, which are:

1857 For a *sin* to be *mortal*, three conditions must together be met: "Mortal sin is sin whose object is grave matter and which is also committed with full knowledge and deliberate consent."(*Reconciliatio et paenitentia*)

1858 *Grave matter* is specified by the Ten Commandments, corresponding to the answer of Jesus to the rich young man: "Do not kill, Do not commit adultery, Do not steal, Do not bear false witness, Do not defraud, Honor your father and your mother." (*Mark 10:19*) The gravity of sin is more or less great: murder is graver than theft. One must also take into account who is wronged: violence against parents is in itself graver than violence against a stranger.

1859 Mortal sin requires *full knowledge* and *complete consent*. It presupposes knowledge of the sinful character of the act, of its opposition to God's law. It also implies a consent sufficiently deliberate to be a personal choice. Feigned ignorance and hardness of heart *(Mark 3:5-6; Luke 16:19-31)* do not diminish, but rather increase, the voluntary character of a sin.
(Holy See, 1997: #1857-1859)

This is how it is for most of the criminals who know what they are doing is wrong but do it anyway.

Criminals justify that crime had to be done as there was no other way to survive. Thus, the truth of the world—all that matters is survival—often dictates criminal actions.

d) Sin is ultimately a distance from God and the criminal suffers from his distance from God.

e) Sin is of the world and the criminal embraces the truth of the world.

f) The criminal world is ancient, built on cultural artifacts from the beginnings of civilization.

g) The criminal world is understood only by its members and understood most completely by its leaders.

h) Punishment for crime is appropriate and penitentially necessary.

Restorative justice encounters this problem—of removing the penitential from justice—except in very minor crimes or civil violations, as it has no provision for punishment in the classical sense of removal and banishment which the prison serves as the modern equivalent.

i) All criminals are redeemable.

Though there have always been Pharisaic movements in the Church to excommunicate most sinners—as during the second century by the purist Hippolytus—there have also always been Popes such as Callistus, the former criminal, to resist them and keep the Church always balanced on the fulcrum of love Christ set as the foundation stone.

36 "Teacher, which is the great commandment in the law?"
37 And he said to him, "You shall love the Lord your God with all your heart, and will all your soul, and with all your mind.
38 This is the great and first commandment.

39 And a second is like it. You shall love your neighbour as yourself. (Matthew 22:36-39)

j) Redeemed criminals, transformed through higher education, training in grassroots organizational management, reconciliation or conversion to Catholicism, and educated in Catholic social teaching—deep knowledge leaders—are the only individuals with the experience, passion, dedication, and criminal world knowledge, able to develop and manage programs that transform other criminals effectively.

The Carceral & the Criminal World

32) One of the most significant developments in the criminal justice system over the past few decades is the impact of the carceral on the criminal world.

Foucault (1975) gave it a cultural importance worth noting:

> Replacing the adversary of the sovereign, the social enemy was transformed into a deviant, who brought with him the multiple danger of disorder, crime and madness. The carceral network linked, through innumerable relations, the two long, multiple series of the punitive and the abnormal.

> The carceral, with its far-reaching networks, allows the recruitment of major

'delinquents'. It organizes what might be called 'disciplinary careers' in which, through various exclusions and rejections, a whole process is set in motion. In the classical period, there opened up in the confines or interstices of society the confused, tolerant and dangerous domain of the 'outlaw' or at least of that which eluded the direct hold of power: an uncertain space that was for criminality a training ground and a region of refuge; there poverty, unemployment, pursued innocence, cunning, the struggle against the powerful, the refusal of obligations and laws, and organized crime all came together as chance and fortune would dictate;... (pp. 299-300)

33) The American prison creates its own environment, its own world, which spreads outward, embracing the terrain where the released wander predatorily, continually reshaping and remaking the criminal world in its own evolving image.

Recent reports, noted by Johnson (2007) pointing to this growing influence:

> A spike in murders in many cities is claiming a startling number of victims with criminal records, police say, suggesting that drug and gang wars are behind the escalating violence. (n.p.)

As the number of criminals moving from the carceral to the outside world, and becoming a critical mass in specific neighborhoods, the influence of the carceral world spreads to the neighborhood, further criminalizing it. Vieraitis, Kovandzic, & Marvell (2007) report:

> [T]he result is that imprisonment causes harm to prisoners. Moreover, the evidence presented here suggests that the general public suffers harm through increases in crime. Although this study does not allow us to draw definitive conclusions about the pathways from prison release to crime rates, research offers several explanations as to how incarceration may increase the likelihood of crime after release. (p. 614)

The more elaborate the prison system is, the deeper Foucault's "dangerous domain", and in California it is perhaps the deepest and most dangerous of all.

34) In California the development of the criminal world related to the prison is strongly congruent and the confused evolution of the California prison—from punishment to rehabilitation and back, and back once more—forlornly retains the uncertainty of the institutional world and the clarity of the criminal world within the carceral.

35) The carceral world looms underneath the criminal world—holding it up as it were—shaping the criminal world's leaders as they pass into and out its steel gates.

Mastering the carceral experience within the maximum security prison is a culturally defining experience determining criminal strength, tenacity, and boldness, much as similarly defined for the non-criminal through mastering the social, athletic, and intellectual rigor of the maximum prestige academy.

And yet the prison is also the most penitential of institutions—so correctly analyzed in its reverential and redeemable components—but rarely seen as that place of exclusion and penance which it is, but more often through the lens of theory critically finding dark motives and capitalistic strategies at work.

36) Transformation has always been considered a desirable aspect of the prison time given to the criminal, and the transformation was to be hoped for as a pure result of prison itself.

For the first century of America's experience with prisons, deeply influenced by religion, it is understood that this occurred more often than not.

Since the 20th century, with its corresponding complexity induced by the majority of humans living in the urban environments of the criminal city; prison induced transformation lost ground as a new meta-narrative extolling criminal exploits became part of the social fabric.

37) In the time we live in, with ethnic, religious, and national myths being folded and blended with the outlaw as hero, a much more convoluted terrain emerges, requiring guides to traverse.

The answer is in the problem.

From a Catholic historic perspective the prison performs a necessary penitential and reformative function, as Skotnicki (2004) notes:

[T]he challenge for the [Catholic] Church is not, at least initially, to question the "why" of the prison, as to provide the answer, given the ancient warrant for the prison, of how penal exclusion can continue to function as the link between justifiable punishment and the desired end of reforming and returning the delinquent to normal social interaction. It is precisely in this regard that images of the prison and the prisoner become essential. In a Catholic anthropology, the nature of the person is to seek God and a harmonious social environment. Spiritual practices, especially contemplation and ritual activity, are essential to the fulfillment of those ends. The theological and moral virtues, habits emanating from the discipline of communal membership and supervision, provide the necessary incentive to keep one on the right path. The growth of confinement reveals that the Church regarded this view of human development as the preferred means for offenders to reacquaint themselves with both the natural ends of human life, as well as the prayer and virtue necessary for their attainment. (pp. 807-808)

38) For the public, the need for the prison is more than the rational reaction of fear to that uncertainty arising from dangerous men, and how to be protected from them. It is also the shutting away of that which is feared, the *other*, which public criminal justice policy too often allows to grow without responsibility while assuming that the real cause of crime is something vague *out there*, rather than predatory thoughts shaping predatory actions; rather a moral decision than an unconscious reaction.

There are over two million people in prisons in the United States representing untold millions of crimes committed, many unaccounted and uncharged, for the criminal as supreme opportunist commits much more than he is ever arrested, charged, and committed for; a danger deep as the ocean.

Murray (2000) reported on these numbers:

The evidence is now heavily weighted toward a substantial effect produced by the aggregate deterrence and incapacitation effects.[of prison] [7] The most recent and most sophisticated analysis, by economist Steven Levitt, takes advantage of the natural experiment offered by prison over-crowding litigation. He finds an estimated net impact of approximately 15 total crimes prevented from adding one additional prisoner for one year.[8] Of these, approximately six would be reported crimes. Multiply six by the number of people in prison in 1997 who would have been on the streets if we had maintained the 1980 imprisonment rate and one gets 6,869,600, or 5,217,600 extra reported index offenses--in the context of the 13 million reported index offenses in 1997 that went into the calculation of the crime rate. Or we could multiply 15 869,600 and come up with 13,044,000 extra total crimes. (np.)

39) In my work as a capacity building consultant to nonprofit organizations, when the strategic discussion concerns the continued utility of a specific course of action, I will bring the discussion back to the founding vision and mission of the organization and from that base, try to determine if indeed, the course of action under discussion is still appropriate.

Regarding the American prison as an organizational entity, let us look at its founding mission and vision, as noted in 1833 by Beaumont & Tocqueville (1964):

> Prisons have been called hospitals for patients laboring under moral disease, but until recently, they have been...of a kind that they ought to be compared rather to the plague-houses in the East, in which every person afflicted with that mortal disorder is sure to perish, and he who is sent there without yet being attacked, is sure to have it....
>
> At last a beginning has been made, and it is a matter of pride to every American that the new penitentiary system has been first established and successfully practiced in his country. That community which first conceived the idea of abandoning the principle of mere physical force even in

respect to prisons, and of treating their inmates as redeemable beings, who are subject to the same principles of action with the rest of mankind, though impelled by vitiated appetites and perverted desires; that community, which after a variety of unsuccessful trials, would nevertheless not give up the principle, but persevered in this novel experiment, until success has crowned its perseverance, must occupy an elevated place in the scale of political or social civilization. (p. 6)

This founding mission has not lost its utility, nor the use of cellular confinement and separation of the criminal from the innocent as a protective and penitential response as well as a redemptive stimulation.

40) The growth of the carceral culture within the criminal world is a dangerous influence which is manifest, and increases as criminalization deepens through carceral influence on cultural reality, again Foucault (1995):

That the prison is not the daughter of laws, codes or the judicial apparatus; that it is not subordinated to the court and the docile or clumsy instrument of the sentences that it hands out and of the results that it would like to achieve; that it is the court that is external and subordinate to the prison. That in the central position that it occupies, it is not alone, but linked to a whole series of 'carceral' mechanisms which seem distinct enough—since they are intended to alleviate pain, to cure, to comfort—but which all tend, like the prison, to exercise a power of normalization...And that ultimately what presides over all these mechanisms is not the unitary functioning of an apparatus or an institution, but the necessity of combat and the rules of strategy. (pp. 307-308)

Combat and the rules of strategy are important capabilities criminals share with the military—of being able to distance yourself from what your emotions are doing and what your body wants to do when confronted with prison life or war. You have to will yourself to act, separating yourself from the urge to panic if you are to survive, whether in prison or battle. How one responds to the carceral is a crucial element in the development of criminal world leadership as is that of the soldier in battle crucial to military leadership development.

41) Criminals who have transformed their lives must speak and help shape the future formation of criminal justice so that it may reach its aspiration of protecting the public and reforming criminals—not currently happening with a 70% recidivism rate—which has little to do with tending to unconsciously generated symptoms, but much to do with transforming suffering into teaching.

As Pope John Paul II taught us in *Salvifici Doloris:*

Even though Paul, in the Letter to the Romans, wrote that "the whole creation has been groaning in travail together until now (8:22)", even though man knows and is close to the sufferings of the animal world, nevertheless what we express by the word "suffering" seems to be particularly *essential to the nature of man.* It is as deep as man himself, precisely because it manifests in its own way that depth which is proper to man, and in its own way surpasses it. Suffering seems to belong to man's transcendence: it is one of those points in which man is in a certain sense "destined" to go beyond himself, and he is called to this in a mysterious way. (#2, italics in the original)

42) The criminal world's leaders understanding is that the criminal is punished for being in congruence with the same reality accepted as true by the punishers.

Within the maximum security prison where criminal world leadership serves time, there exists a long-term solitude-generating contemplation, intimately woven through the Catholic pursuit of spiritual perfection noted by Maritain (1960):

We are here, we believe, in the presence of a central truth. What is principal in the New Law, Saint Thomas Aquinas teaches, is the grace of the Holy Spirit operating in hearts. It is accordingly to internal and invisible reality that major importance has henceforth passed. This law of

41

interiorization, which is characteristic of the New Testament, does not apply only to moral life, where henceforth it is interior movements and their purity which counts first. It applies also to worship itself. (p. 14)

43) For the criminal prior to transformation, this contemplation revolves around the purity of their attachment to the truth of the criminal world, their life in the city of men, most dreadfully realized in the prison itself.

The prison is the truth of the city of men writ hard, writ clearly in steel and stone that none can misunderstand its moment nor its animating core reality.

This lays unconsciously under the day thoughts of most whose work calls them to develop policy around the prison and criminal world—and the politics around prisons are strong—but in the continual struggle around their use and purpose, the thoughts of St. Benedict, which helped shape the use of cell confinement in the West, are enlightening, as noted by Skotnicki (2006):

> What distinguishes the Benedictine Rule in the development of the prison in the West is not its novelty as much as the deliberate attention Benedict devotes to the meaning of cellular confinement, its spiritual and psychological dimension, its peril and its promise...Therefore, the abbot is charged to tread the wise line between a curative penitential medicine and a crushing

experience, where the offender is "devoured by too much sorrow." (pp.90-91)

44) Over the past 70 or 80 years in this country, since the depression of the 1930's, a criminal culture has developed in the country which has become so impenetrable, in terms of changing it, that attempts by criminal rehabilitation practitioners are—and statistics bear this out—a dismal failure.

Attempting to describe this world for those practitioners so that they can find success in it is probably not a fruitful avenue at this moment in rehabilitative history, but the development of reformed criminals, who are cultural leaders, to advance their education and training in helping other criminals transform their lives, would be.

The Criminal City

**I AM THE WAY INTO THE CITY OF WOE,
I AM THE WAY INTO ETERNAL PAIN.
I AM THE WAY TO GO AMONG THE LOST.**

(Dante Alighieri's *Inferno* III: 1-3)

45) The criminal city is the city of men—first mentioned in Genesis—when going to dwell "as a fugitive on the earth at the east side of Eden", after killing Abel and being sent out by God as a vagabond, Cain had children "and he built a city."

Ellul (1970) reflecting on this wrote:

Cain has built a city. For God's Eden he substitutes his own, for the goal given to his life by God, he substitutes a goal chosen by himself—just as he substituted his own security for God's...The city is called Enoch. "Enoch" means "initiation" or "dedication" Cain dedicates a new world. (p. 5-6)

Abel leaves no children as this is not to be a world of righteous men by blood, only by action; for it is only Cain's line that survives of the first sons and his line is that of the prince of this world, the true father of all cities.

46) The city is a metaphor of predatory human behavior—founded by the first predatory human— where, piling on top of one another with the alpha human in the pyramidical penthouse, it vividly portrays the materialism driving its life, where struggling for money is struggling for life, and struggle is marked by predation, noted by Mumford (1964):

> Though the crowds on Fifth Avenue bear witness to the intense and varied life that the great city offers, the vices, perversions, corruptions, parasitisms, and lapses of function increase disproportionately: so that Parasitopolis turns into Patholopolis, the city of mental, moral, and bodily disorders, and finally terminates in Necropolis, the City of the Dead. (p. 340)

In some traditions, the city equals the underworld, as Frazer (1959) notes:

> *Melqarth.* The name would appear to mean "King of the city...W. F. Albright has suggested...that "city" is here the conventional euphemism for the underworld, and that Melqarth is therefore simply an epithet for the god of that realm. For "city" = "underworld" in Sumerian and Semitic literature, see K. Tallquist,...(p. 394)

47) The first criminal founded the first city of men and it is from that beginning and within those precincts that the truth of the world has grown, forming the criminal city.

From the truths of the prince of the world, criminals see what is proclaimed and respond, acting boldly, appropriating the goods of men and relishing the corrupted life animating the criminal city.

The very heart of the city of men—the criminal city—is the prison and the criminal's carceral eyes sees the proclamations of greatness given to leaders in the world who violate their own precepts openly and whose fortune and fame have also been built upon deceit and crime, but whose wealth ensures greatness within the criminal city.

Would a criminal then become a fool and not steal and lie if the truth of the world is the only truth he knows? For he has not yet comprehended the great and certain truths of the Catholic Church resonating through the centuries since its birth on the shoulders of Peter from the blessing of Christ.

48) To move from the criminal city, the beginning of transformation and redemption, the Gospel teaches what lies in store for us:

> If the world hates you, know that it has hated me before it hated you. If you were of the world, the world would love its own; but because you are not of the world, but I chose you out of the world, therefore the world hates you. (John 15:18-19)

The criminal will not move from the comfortable confines of the criminal city he knows, to the unknown city hated by the world, except in the company of friends—reformed criminals—who've traveled the path before him.

49) The truth of the unknown city of human aspiration lies close to the hidden heart, as St. Augustine teaches:

> There was indeed on earth, so long as it was needed, a symbol and foreshadowing image of this city, which served the purpose of reminding men that such a city was to be, rather than making it present; and this image was itself called the holy city, as a symbol of the future city, though not itself the reality. Of this city which served as an image, and of that free city it typified, Paul writes to the Galatians in these terms: "Tell me, ye that desire to be under the law, do ye not hear the law?"(*The City of God*, Book XV: II)

50) Rimbaud (1991) in his benighted search for enlightenment through degradation, describes the criminal in the world:

> A while back, if I remember right, my life was one long party where all hearts were open wide, where all wines kept flowing.
>
> One night, I sat Beauty down on my lap— And I found her galling—And I roughed her up.
>
> I armed myself against justice.
>
> I ran away, O witches, O misery, O hatred, my treasure's been turned over to you!
>
> I managed to make every trace of human hope vanish from my mind. I pounced on every joy like a ferocious animal eager to strangle it.
>
> I called for executioners so that, while dying, I could bite the butts of their rifles. I called for plagues to choke me with sand, with blood. Bad luck was my god. I stretched out in the muck. I dried myself in the air of crime. And I played tricks on insanity. (p. 5)

51) The sense that restraint causes repression—perhaps the founding idea of the 1960's—comes straight from the pagans, and a related quote from an article, part of a symposium on Pope Benedict XVI's Encyclical *Deus Caritas Est* (numbers in parentheses refer to the section in the encyclical) by Schindler (2006):

> The Greeks as well as other cultures linked eros with a kind of "divine madness" or intoxication—see the fertility cults with their sacred prostitution, for example—and thus celebrated eros "as divine power, as fellowship with the divine" (4). The Old Testament firmly opposed this form of religion, "combating it as a perversion of religiosity." (4). But the Old Testament did so, not because it rejected eros, but on the contrary because "this counterfeit divinization of eros actually strips it of its dignity and dehumanizes it" (4)—the prostitutes in the temple, for example, were used as instruments and thus exploited. The point, then, is that an "intoxicated and undisciplined eros...is not an ascent in "ecstasy" toward the divine but a fall, a degradation of man" (4). (p. 349)

52) A strong indictment of the foundational formative praxis of the culture of the United States was delivered by Alexander Solzhenitsyn in 1983:

> The same kind of defect, the flaw of a consciousness lacking all divine dimension, was manifested after World War II when the West yielded to the satanic temptation of the nuclear umbrella. It was equivalent to saying: Let's cast off our worries, let's free the younger generation from its duties and

obligations, let's make no effort to defend ourselves, to say nothing of defending others—let's stop our ears to the groans emanating from the East, and let us live instead in the pursuit of happiness. If danger should threaten us, we shall be protected by the nuclear bomb; if not, then let the world be burned in hell for all we care. The pitifully helpless state to which the contemporary West has sunk is in large measure due to this fatal error; the belief that the defense of peace depends not on stout hearts and steadfast men, but solely on the nuclear bomb. (Ericson & Mahoney (2006) p. 578)

For too much of our history and for too much of our criminal justice system, the prison has served as too much of a model of the nuclear bomb and mutually assured destruction has come with it.

Liberation Theology

53) This important movement in the Church, which began in Latin America, while focusing attention on the plight of the poor, deviated significantly from Church teaching and played a role in the revolutionizing of criminal leaders. It was corrected through the work of the Congregation of the Doctrine of the Faith (CDF) in its Instructions of 1984, 1986, and the 2006 Notification on doctrinal errors in two of the books by Father Jon Sobrino, SJ, one of the intellectual leaders of liberation theology. It has played an unfortunately large and very distractive role in the development of the social justice movement in the United States, in particular with its too strong reliance on the tenets of Marxism rather than of Christianity.

The fallacy embedded in the heart of liberation theology is noted by the CDF in its instruction on the works of Fr. Sobrino (2006):

> The ecclesial foundation of Christology may not be identified with "the Church of the poor", but is found rather in the apostolic faith transmitted through the Church for all generations. The theologian, in his particular vocation in the Church, must continually bear in mind that theology is the science of the faith. Other points of departure for theological work run the risk of arbitrariness and end in a misrepresentation of the same faith. (#2)

This focus on the poor has helped create a political slant to much of the work around social justice in the Church and, rather than helping the marginal as it is meant to do, it actually hurts them by allowing an idea that social conditions are responsible for their predicament rather than personal choices.

It also has tended to set up an adversarial relationship between poor and rich which is harmful to both, and directly contrary to the essential Catholic message of loving and praying for our neighbor.

54) Liberation theology replaced the spiritual core of the Church's teaching focused on changing the individual heart with a material one, focused on changing the structure of the state by taking the Church's care for the poor and conflating the Church's message of liberation from the oppression of sin with the Marxist message of liberation from oppressive social structure.

Liberation theology makes the same mistake as the Catholic monarchists—that the gospel is worldly—which breaks completely from the clear truth Christ gave us in the gospel of Matthew:

> 15. Then the Pharisees went and took counsel how to entangle him in his talk. 16. Teacher, we know that you are true, and teach the way of God truthfully, and care for no man; for you do not regard the position of men. 17. Tell us, then, what you think. Is it lawful to pay taxes to Caesar, or not? 18. But Jesus, aware of their malice, said, "Why put me to the test, you hypocrites? 19. Show me the money for the tax" And they brought him a coin. 20. And Jesus said to them, "Whose likeness and inscription is this?" 21. They said, "Caesar's." Then he said to them, "Render therefore to Caesar the things that are Caesar's and to God the things that are God's." (Matthew 22: 15-21 RSV)

54) The things of this world—most implicitly including the material realization of politics—are of Caesar, are of the prince of this world, while the spiritual force informing and animating them are of God, are of the King of Heaven.

For example: the Church will not correctly call for the state to obtain permission from it prior to passing a law outlawing abortion, but it will always call for the state to legislate the outlawing of abortion.

It is about free will, free choice. We are born with it, it is hard-wired into us, it is why the criminal always chooses to be a criminal or not.

While the internal criminal world is essentially congruent with capitalism and family values, the external actors who claim to speak for the criminal world are largely representatives of Marxist and statist values.

Recently, the emergence of external actors whose perspective is somewhat more congruent is seen in the faith-based organizations.

55) The development we hope to encourage is that of a transformation of criminal world leadership who will speak for themselves, freed from:

> The fact that atheism and the denial of the human person, his liberty and rights, are at the core of the Marxist theory. This theory, then, contains errors which directly threaten the truths of the faith regarding the eternal destiny of individual persons. Moreover, to attempt to integrate into theology an analysis whose criterion of interpretation depends on this atheistic conception is to involve oneself in terrible contradictions. What is more, this misunderstanding of the spiritual nature of the person leads to a total subordination of the person to the

collectivity, and thus to the denial of the principles of a social and political life which is in keeping with human dignity. (Congregation of the Doctrine of the Faith, (1984) # VII: 9)

However, here there lies one important danger to avoid. We must ensure that our focus on the transformed criminal, as perhaps the most marginalized of the poor, does not fall into the error liberation theology did, noted by the Congregation (1984):

But the "theologies of liberation", which reserve credit for restoring to a place of honor the great texts of the prophets and of the Gospel in defense of the poor, go on to a disastrous confusion between the 'poor' of the Scripture and the 'proletariat' of Marx. In this way they pervert the Christian meaning of the poor, and they transform the fight for the rights of the poor into a class fight within the ideological perspective of the class struggle. (IX:10)

We must go beyond liberation theology by still fighting to change the system that brutalizes human beings, but as Peter guides us, by writing—praying—speaking—walking the talk.

Part Two: Catholic Criminal Reentry

Those who have suffered injustice are often best suited to advocate for justice.

Formation & Transformation

56) In the process of criminal transformation, the social teaching of the Church and the relationship it creates with the Magisterium, will often come to play the very important transformational role community often plays.

The social teaching becomes the community wherein the contemplative leader refreshes himself, as the liturgy feeds him.

57) The difficulty with the evangelical approach to criminal transformation is that it is counter to the internal motivation of criminals which is bold rebelliousness; strongly self-centered to the point of pursuing criminal acts which, by their nature, involve those attributes of self-will precluding a bending to evangelical exhortation.

The social teaching approach introduces concepts which are actually very congruent to the criminal's view of himself, while critical of the very same worldly institutions he often sees allied against him; and most importantly, stresses a calm and still small voice approach rather than the salemanistic exhortation.

There is also around the exhortative approach a scent of the coercive, the Elmer Gantry like rock-ribbed persuasion built upon a vision of ever-lasting hell and damnation.

Coercive techniques may suppress crime, and in the case of imprisonment, certainly do; but they are virtually worthless for transformation.

58) Getting to the social teaching—in addition to calling for voluntary action—requires a clear, concise explanation of the truth of the Catholic Church, and what ultimately decided it for me was a series of facts beginning with the positions of the world's major religions founders.

Of the founders of the great religions of the world, only one founder proclaimed himself God—rather than a prophet or an enlightened man—whose Godhood was extensively substantiated by contemporary witnesses.

The others are founded upon the name of a man, and I did not see how a religion, whose defined role is to direct us to knowledge of God, could proclaim truths from any other source than God himself.

I chose to believe that Jesus Christ, the founder of the Catholic Church, founded the religion whose primary purpose is the presentation of the knowledge of God and that he is the man who claimed he was God.

Hilderbrand (2007) expressed it thusly:

> Among all the religious founders, Christ is the only one who said I AM THE TRUTH. Neither Buddha, nor Moses, nor Mohammed have dared utter such words. This assertion can only be validly pronounced by God himself. This is why

Roman Catholics gratefully accept the official teaching of Holy Church, because Christ gave the keys to Peter, and that She alone has the fullness of revelation. (p. 27)

Further, in Christ's proclamation of himself as God, he established his Church upon the rock of Peter and the gates of hell should not prevail against it, and the Catholic Church stands still, buffeted yes, shook to its very core many times yes, but still stands, the pilgrim church.

So, this was my first step, accepting the truth of a man who said he was God and had founded a Church which still stood.

59) And now we come to the teaching, the social teaching of the Church—of the Kingdom of God—that great body of work that has passed down to us from the beginning, through the old covenant into the new.

Beginning at Sinai, noted by Charles (1998):

The law given at Sinai outlines a social order, primitive by modern reckoning, but one sound in ethical essentials: worship of Yahweh is its focal point, justice its basis and love its inspiration....Yet though the law was for the people in general, the Decalogue especially speaks to the individual; the community, important though it was, did not dominate. The law demanded a personal response, the acceptance of personal moral responsibility for one's choices, which was the key to social solidarity. All were bound by the same law of love and its exact

requirements; there was a real basis for social coherence and mutual trust. None was above the law, even the most powerful.
(p. 12-13)

And this justice, this solidarity, moves down through the history of the Church, speaking out for the respect of the dignity of all human beings under God, protecting the dignity even of the criminal, virtually from the beginning.

60) The development of the Magisterium through the expression of the papal encyclical is about as clear a development of how things should be in the world, as the chronicles of the world are about it as it is.

The city of God and the city of men. One clings to us and one calls to us, and in our striving toward transformation we need support.

We have the support of our immediate family, but the Magisterium of the Church can become the community from which we draw our strength, where we can retreat to when suffering, seek advice when confused, and find solace when troubled.

61) In my work, I've learned that the path to transformation exists in and goes through the city of man, which Augustine reminded us is the city created by Cain, the first criminal, and whose ruler is the prince of this world.

And it is a narrow path, beset on all sides by the great temptations of the prince's world, which we see even our sacred priests struggling to resist.

It is a path through our interior life and emanating from our interior life, particularly if our interiority is strongly built on the sacraments, continual prayer and study.

Love illuminates the path, as we have been taught. It is the great commandment, the divine way, and the great light on the path.

Transformation is an interior process and this interior relationship with the Magisterium is now, on account of web-based technology and access to global resources, able to be reinforced and developed with the help of the entire universe of human knowledge.

I have found the deep interiority of the Tridentine Mass to be of great benefit, where the knee is bent and the head is bowed, and alone in my silence with the priest and the Latin I am part of the sacrifice in a profound way and all of the works which go to make up the social teaching are presented to me weekly through the readings and the prayers from so long ago.

62) The social teaching originates, as Fr. Charles (1998) writes:

> The sources of the teaching are fourfold, forming an integrated whole.
>
> 1. The teaching of the scriptures on social ethics.
> 2. The apostolic tradition, that is the relevant teaching of the Fathers and Doctors of the Church, the decisions and directives of councils and Popes, especially the Popes since 1878, the witness of the Saints and martyrs, and the writings of approved

theologians and philosophers on social ethics.

3. The experience of the Church and her members throughout her history, in different cultures and social, political and economic systems.

4. The relevant findings of the human and social sciences. (p. xiii)

The larger body of Catholic thought that makes up the social teaching originated from before creation, was carved in stone at Sinai, was refined by the Sermon on the Mount, was preached throughout the ancient world by the Apostles and was recorded in the New Testament.

It is centered on the sacredness of the human being and the eternal nature of the associated rights, responsibilities, and duties of human beings created by God in their relations with one another and in the societies we create to live and act together in this world.

It tells us to be humble, kind, loving, and in a tremendous enrichment of the Sinai covenant, teaches us that even to harbor anger in our heart towards our enemy is to be judged for killing:

21: You have heard that it was said to them of old: Thou shalt not kill. And whosoever shall kill, shall be liable to the judgment.

22. But I say to you, that whosoever is angry with his brother, shall be liable to the judgment. (Matt. 5:21-22)

From this, and through the centuries of turmoil, of dissolving empires, of the barbaric hordes sweeping through Europe and North Africa, and of the Babel-like splitting from her, the Catholic Church held clear to the central themes of human dignity and respect due each individual person from before the foundations of the world were set.

63) The family, the crux of human development, was formed and created as the consensual norm it is through the influence of the Catholic Church through the ages, as noted by Wilson (1993):

> By the end of the Middle Ages, something like the consensual family of today had become the norm in Christendom, sanctioned by religion and law as well as by custom and preference.
>
> Just how that change occurred is not clearly understood and, given the absence of much in the way of a written record, may always remain somewhat puzzling. But a number of scholars now agree that the Catholic Church played a key role in this development.
> (p. 202)

64) St. Callistus, St. Augustine, and all of the fathers and doctors of the Church, formed and shaped the teaching through the centuries.

In the modern era, the work was collected in the papal encyclicals, beginning with that of 1891,

Pope Leo XIII's *Rerum Novarum* (On the Rights and Duties of Capital and Labor).

This was an important intellectual shaping of the labor movement, which had seen Labor Day designated as a holiday in New York on September 5, 1882, and the national designation by act of Congress in June of 1894, making the first Monday in September their day.

Crime Belongs to Caesar, Criminals to God

65) While the response to the crimes criminals commit in the world belongs to Caesar and there is no choice in the matter; the response to the individual human being who is the criminal, his transformation and redemption—which is purely a matter of choice—belongs to God.

The social and legal structures the state creates around human beings are not as important as the human being. What is defined as crime and how it is to be responded to by the state is the concern of Caesar as the state, but the Church is called to inform those decisions of the state through the knowledge implicit within its social teaching.

66) The criminal world in the United States began to become a well-organized and coherent entity during the generation between World War I and World War II. By the period between the Korean War and the Vietnam War—wars being appropriate markers for its development—it had become a large, powerful, and virtually permanent aspect of American culture.

This is not a situation unique to this country or this time. During medieval times the underworld was well developed in Europe, as it was in Regency England. What is different is how the carceral world has become the prime cultural shaper of the criminal world, developing criminal world leadership unprecedented in our country.

What this means in terms of developing policies able to actually address criminal behavior with any hope of redemption and transformation, is that transformed criminal leadership—the only resource with deep understanding of the criminal world—must become involved in the transformative process.

One of the most important reasons for that involvement is that the development and management of traditional rehabilitation efforts is—as some studies are clearly revealing—actually enhancing criminal behavior rather than reducing it.

67) Involving those who are part of the process in the leadership is similar to the business world's effective use of organizational development knowledge, ideas growing from, among others, Mary Parker Follett's concept of power-with rather than power-over.

What works in the business world facilitating the organizational aspects of transformation however, is not what works in the spiritual. In the spiritual we are called to revealed truth, absolute, clear, and final; truth which all human beings—including criminals—are hard-wired to seek.

That spiritual call is to the Catholic Church.

68) Recently Pope Benedict (2007) traveled to Brazil and while there, spoke to the recovering drug addicts at the Farm of Hope:

> 3. "Behold, I stand at the door and knock; if anyone hears my voice and opens the door, I will come in to him and eat with him, and he with me" (Revelation 3:20). These are divine words which penetrate to the depths of our souls and shake us at our deepest roots.
>
> At some stage in people's lives, Jesus comes and gently knocks at the hearts of those properly disposed. Perhaps for you, he did this through a friend or a priest, or, who knows, perhaps he arranged a series of coincidences which enabled you to realize that you are loved by God. Through the institution which has welcomed you, the Lord has given you this opportunity for physical and spiritual recovery, so vital for you and your families. In turn, society expects you to spread this precious gift of health among your friends and all the members of the community.
>
> You must be Ambassadors of hope! Brazil's statistics concerning drug abuse and other forms of chemical dependency are very high. The same is true of Latin America in general. I therefore urge the drug-dealers to reflect on the grave harm they are inflicting on countless young people and on adults from every level of society: God will call you to

account for your deeds. Human dignity cannot be trampled upon in this way. The harm done will receive the same censure that Jesus reserved for those who gave scandal to the "little ones", the favourites of God (cf. Matthew 18:7-10)."

Lighting the Path

69) Transformed Criminals: The work of the Lampstand Foundation is specifically directed towards those transformed criminals, who are able, through inclination, redemption, education, and skill, to become a grassroots organizational leader who can generate the transformation of other criminals.

For optimal use, it is important to understand for whom the work of Lampstand is intended, from where those leaders would come, and what identifiers would reveal them to us.

Our work is directed to penitential criminals who are Catholic or potential converts who, because of their leadership in the criminal world, will have significant success and impact in the work of criminal transformation.

70) Those offenders, whose crimes are such that they would be included in this Gospel message of Christ, do not occupy those positions of leadership in the criminal or carceral world:

> 5. And he that shall receive one such child in my name, receiveth me.
> 6. But he that shall scandalize one of these little ones that believe in me, it were better

for him that a mill-stone were hanged about his neck, and that he were drowned in the depth of the sea.

7. Wo to the world because of scandals. For it must needs be that scandals come: but, nevertheless wo to that man by whom the scandal cometh.

(Matthew 18: 5-7, Douay Rheims)

71) Catholic Audience: The path being lighted can only be traveled by reformed criminals who are Catholics, and this work is created for them. The effectiveness of criminal transformative teaching is dependent upon a deep understanding of the principles of Catholic social teaching, which is only possible by being devoutly Catholic. Merkle (2004) notes:

> It takes a converting and transformed heart not only to carry out the imperatives of [Catholic] social teaching but to understand its logic in the first place. For this reason, the social teaching of the Church is only fully understood within the matrix of living the life of the Church, the sacraments, prayer, community, and doctrine. Social teaching requires a social conscience to be understood, and such a conscience is fed by service, prayer, worship, and the example of community one finds within the Church. While it is true that social teaching is written also to all people of good will, its logic, and practice finds an echo in those who share

Church values, albeit from different supports and practice. (p. 17)

72) Criminal: From our perspective, we use the term criminal to refer to those individuals who committed crimes for money—professional criminals—to whom crime was a way of life and prison time an occupational hazard. We are also speaking of professional criminals who have spent at least five years in a maximum security prison—the benchmark of professional criminality after arrest and conviction.

It is from these criminals that the leadership in the carceral world comes and it is from them that effective reentry leadership will also emerge.

Each population has a certain percentage from which effective leadership usually emerges and it is no different within the criminal world.

There are certain characteristics and criminal experiences that serve as the foundation of criminal world leadership and others that preclude someone from being perceived as a leader.

Criminal world leaders are not informers, do not commit crimes against children and women, nor allow themselves to be victimized by others, particularly in prison.

There are many people who have served time in one type of prison honor farm, medical facility, or minimum or medium security prison, who have developed and manage prisoner rehabilitation efforts, but have not developed the leadership within the criminal world which give them either the stature or gravitas to become an effective rehabilitation practitioner.

73) Transformation: Criminals become part of the communal community when they make the choice to transform themselves, to create from within a different person than what they were previously; a person whose motivation is based on eternal truth, only found in the Catholic Church, the City of God, than the truth of the world, the city of man. Rehabilitation is not a proper word for this process as it implies a return to something that previously existed—criminals are by and large born into the criminal world—and sets the entire criminal transformation process on the incorrect intellectual setting, which is partly the reason for its continued failure in the United States.

74) Communal Reentry: The community being reentered is the community of the Catholic Church—triumphant, suffering, and militant—and for transformed criminals involved with their apostolate of transforming others, it is the only community, beyond their family, needed.

Traditionally reentry is a three year period after release from prison when about 70% of criminals in the United States return to prison. Reentry is often used to designate those released from any type of criminal justice sanctioning, probation, parole, jail or prison release, but we use it specifically in reference to those professional criminals released from a maximum security prison (or a transitional prison after serving the bulk of their time in a maximum security facility).

We also use a ten year period of reentry as it allows for the fuller development of transformative behavior—and a more accurate reflection of return statistics— than the relatively short three year period does.

75) The reason Catholics need to be involved in transformation and reentry is because Catholicism is the only faith based on truth, a solid and robust enough truth—eternal truth, real truth, truthful truth—to provide a strong enough contrast to the truth of the world—sense truth, perceived truth, relative truth, truth-built-on-lies truth—to attract criminals, who whatever their faults, seeing things incorrectly based on what it is they know is not one of them.

This truth of the Church was reaffirmed by the Vatican in June 2007:

> Christ "established here on earth" only one Church and instituted it as a "visible and spiritual community", that from its beginning and throughout the centuries has always existed and will always exist, and in which alone are found all the elements that Christ himself instituted. "This one Church of Christ, which we confess in the Creed as one, holy, catholic and apostolic [...]. This Church, constituted and organised in this world as a society, subsists in the Catholic Church, governed by the successor of Peter and the Bishops in communion with him". (n. p.)

76) Within the Catholic Magisterium, the social teaching, that body of documents primarily built upon papal encyclicals, tradition, and scripture, is the robust story that destroys the lie the world's truth is built on, the world truth criminals have built their lives on.

The knowledge about the city of men—the criminal city—and the City of God, so precisely presented to us in the Gospels, is amplified through the works of the early church fathers, and in the case of the criminal who builds his life on the truth of the city of men rather than the City of God, by St. Augustine (426 A.D.) who teaches us:

> This race we have distributed into two parts, the one consisting of those who live according to man, the other of those who live according to God. And these, we also mystically call the two cities, or the two communities of men, of which the one is predestined to reign eternally with God, and the other to suffer eternal punishment with the devil...
>
> Of these two first parents of the human race, then, Cain was the first-born, and he belonged to the city of men; after him was born Abel, who belonged to the city of God. For as in the individual the truth of the apostle's statement is discerned , "that is not first which is spiritual, but that which is natural, and afterward that which is spiritual," (Cor. Xv.46) whence it comes to past that each man, being derived from a condemned stock, is first born of Adam evil and carnal, and becomes good and spiritual only afterwards when he is grafted into Christ by regeneration; so was it in the human race as a whole...Not indeed, that

every wicked man shall be good, but that no one will be good who was not first of all wicked; but the sooner any one becomes a good man, the more speedily does he receive this title; and abolish the old name in the new. (p. 478-479)

77) The catechesis of the criminal brought through the social teaching—Catholic doctrine presented in universal terms—works, because within the social teaching is found the unbroken line of truth that connects one to the beginning of creation and the institution housing it, still remaining true to those ancient roots; something that can be said of no other institution on earth.

The criminal will find that Christ specifically speaks to him and his entire sinning world, who has been deceived into believing the truth of the world, and living by the rules of men in the city of men, which the criminal does more boldly than the rest.

78) Being able to speak from brotherly love, the reformed criminal—who grows to deeply enjoy many aspects of his criminal life—knows the failure of active love in the oft quoted "love the sinner, hate the sin" in a life where identification with the sin is often deep.

The process, for non-Catholics, of coming into the Church, is not the instantaneous events Slevin (2007) notes:

> Interested inmates at Newton Correctional Facility in Iowa receive teaching material that declares: "Criminal behavior is a

manifestation of an alienation between the self and God. Acceptance of God and Biblical principles results in cure through the power of the Holy Spirit. Transformation happens through an instantaneous miracle; it then builds the prisoner up with familiarity of the Bible." (p. A-13)

Instead, it is a strenuous year-long process of catechesis that represents the true ritual of transformation every redemptive criminal (and every convert to Catholicism) need traverse, ending ultimately with the sacramental forgiveness of all sins.

The Church dwells in the interior of man—in the communion with Christ—not in the community of men, and through its interiority guides the walking of the talking.

79) For centuries the criminal, like Cain, could be banished, or voluntarily disappear, begin again as a new person, even during recent times and recent criminal lives that possibility existed, but no more.

Now all are connected and all crimes rest on the knowing conscience of the world and the only rebirth is through baptism.

Now, we all come in our ancient ways to fields love alone blooms.

Today, even outside of prison, the criminal is panopticized, backlit, fully visible, only requiring the eye of the examiner gazing upon the digital data summoned from the great maw and storehouse of the digital world.

Contemplating this, even if having begun an internal transformation, often renders change moot. Labeled and exposed the criminal too often accepts reality and returns to crime, or turns to a friend.

Teaching from Suffering

80) The preeminent example of teaching from suffering is the cross, and one of the Church's greatest teachers about the mysteries of the cross is St. John of the Cross (1991) who developed some of his finest work while suffering the isolation of imprisonment, noted by his translator:

> His accusers [for supposedly violating the ordinances of his order] locked him first in the monastery prison, but at the end of two months, for fear of an escape, they moved him to another spot, a room narrow and dark, without air or light except for whatever filtered through a small slit high up in the wall. The room was six feet wide and ten feet long [almost exactly the size of modern prison cells]. There John remained alone, without anything but his breviary, through the terribly cold winter months and the suffocating heat of summer. Added to this were the floggings, fasting on bread and water, wearing the same bedraggled clothes month after month without being washed— and the lice. [St] Teresa wrote to the king and pleaded that for the love of God he order Fray John set free at once.

In the midst of this deprivation, Fray John was seeking relief by composing poetry in his mind, leaving to posterity some of the greatest lyric stanzas in Spanish literature— among them a major portion of *The Spiritual Canticle.* (p. 18)

81) And Jurgens (1970) quotes from the *Didache*—written in A.D. 140—the early use of confinement to teach men how to live according to the commandments:

> Blessed is the man who gives according to the commandment; for he is without blame. Woe to him that takes. Yet, if he takes because he is in need, he is blameless; but if he be not in need, he shall give an account of the why and the wherefore of his taking. He will be put under constraint so that he may be examined closely as to what he did; and he will not come out from there until he has paid the last farthing. (p. 1)

82) Acknowledging the value inherent within the suffering from imprisonment that can deeply enrich the process of criminal transformation is one of the most important aspects of Lampstand's work.

Without prison suffering—gateway to the penitential process—corresponding to the suffering of the criminal's victims, the professional criminal has not built the foundation for the future work of transformation.

The movement towards the penitential is the movement of the natural law growing within us.

Within Catholic history the use of imprisonment, and the benefits of the suffering it has generated, have brought us precious flowers of knowledge.

83) Catholic criminal transformative work should be supported by Catholic institutional resources until its effectiveness is determined. The optimal sought would be government support of faith-based efforts for a specified trial period, determine which is most effective and direct more funding there.

One major benefit of working with criminals in determining the effectiveness of transformative programs is that criminal records are available through criminal justice data bases, unlike virtually any other segment of social work.

Using the reentry period of three years—or ten years as our marker—we can tell if involvement with our suggested faith-based program works by looking at arrest records over the three or ten year period.

The constitutional prescriptions allowing this can be built upon the same freedom of religion foundation currently allowing single-faith service and ritual within prisons.

The current legal issues surrounding the use of faith-based efforts will go on, but it is in the public interest to determine what is effective with reentering prisoners, as major public safety issues and large sums of public money are at stake.

We might have as much at stake in this effort and determining what works as we do in the military action embarked upon by our national government. We should consider if it is within national public priorities to be expending proportionately appropriate evaluative resources in determining program success with criminals at home, as we are with terrorists abroad.

84) Beirne & Messerschmidt (2000) share an interesting perspective related to the concept of reformed criminals becoming thought leaders in the criminal reformation field during a discussion of the ideas of one of the founders of sociological criminology, Emile Durkheim (1858-1917) and they noted:

> For Durkheim, crime is useful because often it is a symptom of individual originality and a preparation for changes in law and morality. He cited the fate of Socrates as an example of crime's utility. Socrates (470-399 B.C.), perhaps the most original of all Greek philosophers, committed the "crime" of independent thought. Having been convicted of not believing in the official gods of the Athenian state and of corrupting the minds of the young, Socrates committed suicide by drinking hemlock. Durkheim suggested that "Socrates' crime served to prepare the way for a new morality and a new faith—one the Athenians...needed [inasmuch as] the traditions by which they had hitherto lived no longer corresponded to the conditions of their existence"...Today's criminal may be tomorrow's philosopher!
> (p. 97)

Perhaps sooner than one thinks.

85) Mother Teresa, who underwent a period of suffering that lasted almost her entire apostolate, can also help us to see the power of the light that comes from the deepest darkness.

The dark night of the soul is life without God, and for some of us, no internal sense that God exists, though happening rarely, even extremely rarely, would be horrible and few would survive it with faith intact, but those who do, such as Mother Teresa, are greater for it, as they have lived that of which Christ spoke, "the faith of a mustard seed", the knowing that you are a child of God, and that with the proper growth to the light, will return home to God for eternity, making this short abode on earth the reality it is.

The Grassroots

86) It is said that Satan, faced with the intrusion of eternal truth into the world, attempts to institutionalize it, thereby ensuring it is ignored by the public.

The leaders of grassroots organizations are the social entrepreneurs of the nonprofit sector. They have discovered an aspect of eternal truth and organized others around it for the good of the community. The community, who needs their passion and commitment, is best served by their being able to keep closely aligned with their core values, vision, and their truth (mission) as they evolve into a community institution.

While one of the goals of all grassroots organizations is—or should be—to become institutionalized to the point that community support becomes a stable given, it is too often precisely the point at which they become much less effective as a mission-driven organization. The truth often gives way to the expediency of becoming stable and solvent.

87) Community transformation emerges from the small, grass-roots organization, through the work of a few committed individuals coming together for a great cause. It is from the grassroots that individual dignity is protected, hope encouraged, and communities strengthened.

The leaders of these organizations are the true inheritors of the voluntary associations of virtue and service to the public good that Benjamin Franklin brought to fruition in colonial America, and Alexis de Tocqueville marveled at in the 19th century in his landmark book, *Democracy in America*.

De Tocqueville came to America in the early 1800's, met with many of the country's founders, and wrote one of the most perceptive books ever written about America. This is part of what he wrote about voluntary associations and America, (Mansfield & Winthrop, 2000)

> Thus the most democratic country on earth is found to be, above all, the one where men in our day have most perfected the art of pursuing the object of their common desires in common and have applied this new science to the most objects. Does this result

from an accident or could it be that there in fact exists a necessary relation between associations and equality? (p. 490)

Among the nobility of the time, of which De Tocqueville was a member, good work was accomplished, when it was, by the nobility coercing others to follow them in the accomplishment of their aims. He had never witnessed common people banding together voluntarily to accomplish social ends and he marveled at it, understanding that it was the basis of democracy.

88) When I think about what defines a grassroots organization, I think back to this initial formation: mission-driven, entrepreneurial, voluntary and community-based. The truly real grassroots organization begins in the heart of one person who has witnessed injustice and wants to remedy it, or been moved by beauty and wants to share it, or gained wisdom and wants to teach others, or transformed the pain of their suffering into the powerful desire of teaching and comforting others.

These leaders often begin without any money, but have an idea to help—in some way—the world they see in front of them. Through their passion and dedication they bring others along with them in their journey of healing and begin the process of transformation.

If they are wise, lucky, and committed, they and the organizations they create, will survive and grow strong, and we will be the richer for their struggles, as they bring their healing service to our troubled world. If they succumb to the lure of financial stability over the purity of their vision and mission, we will ultimately be the lesser as their promise of healing becomes the maintenance of the status quo.

89) Eric Hoffer, a longshoreman who worked in San Francisco for many years, wrote a book called *The True Believer*. His thesis was that the true believer, who strive for a belief to the exclusion of all else, are to be feared for they are the soil from which political and religious fanaticism springs. There is much truth in this, but at the same time, it is the true believer who drives the social mission onward. It is they whose passion and true beliefs drive a social agenda that enriches us all.

The role of the grassroots organization is to shake the establishment, it is to be true to a mission of truth, to venerate that truth and express it through love for those who need help, through justice in honor of their suffering, through sharing beauty and the joy of artistic discovery, and through community building in pursuit of the transformation of the great human heart of the commons, and a most proper place, perhaps the only place, for the transformation of criminals.

OD, The Natural Language of Nonprofits

90) One of the more important disciplines the deep knowledge leader can study to increase his capability to develop and manage an effective grassroots nonprofit criminal transformative organization, is Organization Development (OD).

Cummins & Worley (2005) define OD:

> Organization development is both a professional field of social action and an area of scientific inquiry. The practice of OD covers a wide spectrum of activities, with seemingly endless variations upon them. Team building with top corporate management, structural change in a municipality, and job enrichment in a manufacturing firm are all examples of OD. Similarly, the study of OD addresses a broad range of topics, including the effects of change, the methods of organizational change, and the factors influencing OD success. (p. 1)

Organization Development (OD) and the mission-driven organizational imperatives of nonprofit criminal transformative organizations (CTOs) share common values and complementary realities.

This congruence represents opportunities for the deep knowledge leadership of criminal transformative organizations and OD practitioners.

Nonprofits, as O'Neill (2002) noted are:

> (1) organizations or institutionalized to some extent, (2) private or not part of government, (3) non-profit-distributing, (4) self-governing, (5) voluntary or noncompulsory and involving some meaningful degree of voluntary participation, and (6) of public benefit (p. 2).

Nonprofits serve the public good, they provide a public service, and they are humanistic by definition.

CTOs are generally grassroots nonprofit organizations who act as organizational change agents transforming criminals and their communities.

In the United States, there are 103,171 human service nonprofit organizations with revenue of $142.3 billion and assets of $209.3 billion. (Nonprofit Almanac, (2007) p. 3)

Within that large group there are probably several hundred that could be classified as CTO's in some way—though I have not found any statistics to provide proof for that assertion—as many deal with some aspect of criminal transformation as part of their related mission work, for instance, an organization that deals with homeless issues will often be dealing with former or current criminals who are homeless.

91) While the deep knowledge leaders of CTOs are driven by their mission, bringing passion and commitment to their cause, they are often lacking in the internal organizational capacity building tools needed for sustainability. The specific tools they are most deficient in are strategic planning, fund development, board & staff development, and communications & marketing, all of which can benefit from an OD perspective.

OD values include humanism, collaboration, cooperation, participation, knowledge of self and

81

awareness of one's impact, empowerment of individuals, groups, and organizations, and social responsibility/sustainability.

CTOs can achieve individual and community transformation most effectively when embracing their own values as applied to their own organizational functioning.

This will affect the governance, strategy, and fund development capability of the board and staff, which directly impacts the mission fulfillment—the core reason for their existence—of the nonprofit organization.

Here is an area where some of the basic techniques of OD can be helpful, such as creating a learning community, using group work to help clients mentor board and staff members, and board members mentor clients. Co-creating an environment where the inherent corrosiveness of the criminal world can be mitigated through the inherent self-responsibility of the board and staff member's world, leading to an organizational culture of mutual learning and healing in a transformative setting.

I have worked with several small CTOs where this inability to connect the staff and board to the criminal world has dramatically affected the ability of the organization to help its criminal client base, particularly in growing to scale and organizational effectiveness.

Individuals with humanistic ideals self-select into both non-profit environments and OD careers, actively choosing settings they feel congruent with. This would indicate that nonprofit staff and board may be open to operating according to OD values, but do not have the exposure or tools. If they did so, they would be modeling and enhancing mission work, and becoming more congruent with the natural language of the nonprofit world.

Individual development, organization development, and development of the social environment cannot be truly separated; they are reciprocal. Many CTOs fail because they haven't transformed themselves.

OD has traditionally been marketed to for-profit organizations but CTOs are more able to realize the values aspirations of OD, and at a higher level of congruency.

The absence of a profit motive creates deeper ground for the enactment of OD and its values. Block (2002) has referred to "organization" as the "construct of an engineer", concerned with problem-solving, and has referred to "development" as the "construct of a healer", concerned with relationships, feeling, and humanity.

The CTO embodies both of these constructs as it is a problem-solving entity which heals.

CTOs—animated by a mission of individual and community transformation—will benefit from discovering a mission of management imbued by values-driven transformation, consistent with the values and practice of OD.

The Grassroots & Criminal Transformation

92) Rehabilitating criminals is big business in America and there are ideas and programs continually being promoted that show some initial success which the federal government then attempts to scale up to national import.

This is a familiar pattern when dealing with criminal rehabilitation and appears doomed to the continual failure it has traditionally been, because of the tendency—most marked in those who develop new programs that do work—to move on from direct service success at the grassroots level to administrative positions at the corporate or governmental level, taking their energy, insight and dedication with them.

There is also a lack of effective succession planning among grassroots nonprofits.

93) Reformed criminals—particularly those who have gained deep knowledge—however, have a level of connection hard to break.

Bornstein (2004) in discussing the motivation of the social entrepreneurs he studied found:

> I heard the same story again and again. Someone had experienced an intense kind of pain that branded them in some way. They said, 'I had to do this. There is nothing else I could do."...

> At some moment in their lives, social entrepreneurs get it into their heads that it is up to them to solve a particular problem. Usually something has been brewing inside for a long time, and at a particular moment in time—often triggered by an event—personal preparedness, social need, and

historical opportunity converge and the person takes decisive action...

From that point on, the social entrepreneurs seem to cut off other options for themselves. Over time, their ideas become more important to them than anything else. Every decision—whom to marry, where to live, what books to read—passes through the prism of their ideas...and society stands to benefit by finding these people, encouraging them, and helping them do what they need to do. (pp. 240-241)

94) Regarding criminal reentry, we certainly have the social need, with 650,000 (and rising) criminals being released annually to the community; and the historical opportunity, with virtually no record of successful reentry programs to help them. The triggering event could be the government and criminal justice professional practitioners asking for the reformed criminals help.

Those who have restored their life can help others restore theirs; the solution is often found within the mirrored image of the problem.

The reformed criminal could begin the process of preparedness by advancing into graduate level college work and organizational management training.

This could also begin to counter—during output—the deadening reality of the relative speechlessness of criminals in their interaction with the criminal justice system during input, noted by Natapoff (2004):

> The United States criminal justice system is shaped by a fundamental absence: Criminal defendants rarely speak. From the first Miranda warnings through trial until sentencing, defendants are constantly encouraged to be quiet and to let their lawyers do the talking. And most do. Over ninety-five percent never go to trial, only half of those who do testify, and some defendants do not even speak at their own sentencing. As a result, in millions of criminal cases often involving hours of verbal negotiations and dozens of pages of transcripts, the typical defendant may say almost nothing to anyone but his or her own attorney. (pp. 1449-1450)

95) A current trend that will only continue to accelerate and which will require even deeper understanding of those who would help criminals transform is the increasing transparency of criminal records.

The *Home News Tribune*, a New Jersey newspaper was the first to allow criminal record searches for free from its website. These searches, which can normally cost from $10 to $50 through the private sector, put public record criminal information online.

This is a good public service, and while it is appropriate for the public to know about the background of criminals it has to deal with through hiring, renting, volunteering with, and attending church with; the public attitudes around being involved with people with criminal records creates another significant hurdle in the reentry process.

The only effective response to this is a public openness about one's past by the criminal transforming his life, and those transformed criminals working in the field will be modeling openness through their behavior as deep knowledge leaders.

Criminals & the Church

96) From the very beginning, criminals played a major role in the Church—the good thief Dismas being an early example—and another was the transformed criminal who became pope, St. Callistus (died 222). His experience-based decree selection caused a severe political break in the Church, but restored its heart of mercy and redemption, when he decreed forgiveness for major sinners after confession and penance, against the wishes of many early Christians. As Craughwell (2006) explains:

> Callistus' brief five-year reign was marked by the virtue he had come to appreciate above all others. He decreed that Christians who had committed fornication or adultery, even Christians who had fallen into heresy, could be restored to full Communion with the Catholic Church once they had confessed their sins and done penance. Pope Callistus' ruling split the Church between orthodox

Catholics who understood that the Church was in the forgiveness business, and more rigid Catholics who felt that certain sins were unforgivable. The leader of the inflexible faction was Hippolytus, a Roman priest and theologian, who knew about Callistus' shameful past and despised him for it. An angry, vindictive man, Hippolytus taught that any Christian who committed even a single mortal sin ought to be driven out of the Church and never permitted to return, no matter how sincerely he or she might repent. (p. 15)

This inflexibility and strict adherence to the language of the Church's law rather than the spirit of it marks some brief moments in the history of the Church, as of all institutions, but none walks the talk as does the Church.

97) Hippolytus, the leader of those who attacked Callistus throughout his papacy was the anti-pope who came back to the Church, eventually becoming one of her fathers.

Hippolytus attacked Callistus with venom, and what struck me reading about his attacks and the ferocity with which they were raised, considering the great admiration most Catholics felt for Callistus, leads to the conclusion that perhaps what most troubled Hippolytus was that Callistus, a common criminal, was getting the honor he felt he, Hippolytus, deserved.

Callistus, as a redeemed criminal, understood better than most that redemption was always possible and Christ's message was, if it was anything, that all could be forgiven.

However, as Pope Callistus allowed many who had committed major sins to return, after proper penance, to the fold of the Church, Hippolytus and his supporters were enraged, feeling even the committing of one major sin precluded future involvement with the Church.

98) The powerful denouement to this wonderful story of two men—one pope and one anti-pope—in the early days of the Church; was that upon being imprisoned for claiming himself as pope in reaction to the acts of Pope Callistus, Hippolytus later redeemed himself, primarily as a result of the same sort of imprisonment once suffered by Callistus, and the knowledge gained from his suffering there.

As Foley & McCloskey (2003) note:

> Hippolytus was a strong defender of orthodoxy, and admitted his excesses by his humble reconciliation. He was not a formal heretic, but an overzealous disciplinarian. What he could not learn in his prime as a reformed and purist, he learned in the pain and desolation of imprisonment. (p. 204)

Callistus, the prodigal son who became pope, fulfilled the inner lesson of the parable noted by Pope Benedict XVI (2007):

> The parable [of the prodigal son] breaks off here; it tells us nothing about the older brother's reaction. Nor can it, because at this

point the parable immediately passes over into reality. Jesus is using these words of the father to speak to the heart of the murmuring Pharisees and scribes who have grown indignant at his goodness to sinners. (p. 209)

Callistus spoke to the heart of the Pharisees of his time with his goodness and forgiveness of sinners they would not forgive.

99) Another early Church leader who spoke out against Pope Callistus' action in readmitting penitential sinners to the Church was Tertullian.

The consequences of Pope Callistus' policy, which also involved some struggle over the primacy of Rome in setting Church policy—in this case for those who had lapsed under persecution—reverberated through the early Church, noted by Whitehead (2000):

> The Roman [Pope's] position on the readmission of those who had lapsed under persecution was endorsed and adopted by Cyprian and by the Church in Africa as a whole...and adopted in Alexandria and Antioch...

> This discipline was a development of the position taken a generation earlier by Pope St. Callistus when he decided, much to Tertullian's disgust, that sins of the flesh earlier held by some to be unforgivable when committed after baptism could be remitted by the Church.

...This was a momentous decision, and the drama of how it was arrived at in the give-and-take between the Churches—and between the factions within the Churches—can barely be covered by the summary we have given here. (pp. 183-184)

100) This continual history of forgiveness and acceptance forms the ground for a significant aspect of our work; developing a case for the use of Catholic social teaching in the transformation of criminals.

In the discussion I had with criminals who were cultural leaders in the criminal world over the twenty years I was involved in that world, one thing usually became clear once we got down to the real reasoning around the decision to become a criminal; "everyone's doing it".

Believing that the upperworld rewards criminal behavior just as much, if not more, than the underworld, the choice to become a criminal is not difficult. It is a matter of either accepting the way the world is, and becoming good at dealing with it, or ignoring it and becoming a fool who is taken advantage of by it.

The institutions that would stand against this truth of the world and present eternal truth, too often show, upon examination, feet of clay.

However, with a presentation of the world of Catholic social teaching through the Magisterium and the Chair of Peter, this misconception can be addressed and the natural human tendency to move to what is true can be reinvigorated.

101) One of the clearest expressions from Peter through the recent centuries that stood against the truth of the world, is that regarding slavery, and Pope Gregory XVI in 1839 wrote this:

It is at these practices that are aimed the Letter Apostolic of Paul III, given on May 29, 1537, under the seal of the Fisherman, and addressed to the Cardinal Archbishop of Toledo, and afterwards another Letter, more detailed, addressed by Urban VIII on April 22, 1639 to the Collector Jurium of the Apostolic Chamber of Portugal. In the latter are severely and particularly condemned those who should dare 'to reduce to slavery the Indians of the Eastern and Southern Indies,' to sell them, buy them, exchange them or give them, separate them from their wives and children, despoil them of their goods and properties, conduct or transport them into other regions, or deprive them of liberty in any way whatsoever, retain them in servitude, or lend counsel, succour, favour and co-operation to those so acting, under no matter what pretext or excuse, or who proclaim and teach that this way of acting is allowable and co-operate in any manner whatever in the practices indicated.

Benedict XIV confirmed and renewed the penalties of the Popes above mentioned in a new Apostolic Letter addressed on December 20, 1741, to the Bishops of Brazil and some other regions, in which he stimulated, to the same end, the solicitude of the Governors themselves. Another of Our Predecessors, anterior to Benedict XIV, Pius II, as during his life the power of the Portuguese was extending itself over New Guinea, sent on October 7, 1462, to a Bishop who was leaving for that country, a Letter in which he not only gives the Bishop himself the means of exercising there the sacred ministry with more fruit, but on the same occasion, addresses grave warnings with regard to Christians who should reduce neophytes to slavery. (n.p.)

102) From the very first, in the stating of the great commandment by Christ:

> 36 Master, which is the great commandment in the law? 37 Jesus said to him: Thou shalt love the Lord thy God with thy whole heart, and with thy whole soul, and with thy whole mind. 38 This is the greatest and first commandment. 39 And the second is like to this: Thou shalt love thy neighbor as thyself. 40 On these two commandments dependeth the whole law and the prophets. (Matthew 22: 36-40 Douay-Rheims)

There is no doubt here that slavery is against God, the Law, and the Prophets, no doubt at all. But Christ was not a revolutionary come to overturn the social structure within which slavery was an accepted part of daily life. He rendered to Caesar that which was Caesars.

Fr. Charles (1998) notes:

The reason why slavery and Christianity were ultimately in conflict was stated by St. Paul. All—Jew and Greek, slave and free, male and female—are one in Jesus Christ (Galatians 3:28). The institution remained, however, because it did not occur to the generality of men that it could be dispensed with; it was too necessary to the maintenance of life as they understood it. (Vol. 1: p. 50)

It is this type of institutional clarity, carried out through time that will resonate with other criminals as it has with me, let alone the multitude of recent converts to Catholicism who have found in the intellectual storehouse of the Church a great call home.

Grassroots Organizations & Subsidiarity

103) In the United States the founding of organizations helping prisoners began with churches, and were primarily managed by the wives of pastors or prominent businessmen who were members of the church.

They were very close to the individual prisoners and criminals they helped as they worked within their church community. Over time these organizations grew and became more professionalized as did the nonprofit sector.

104) By the middle of the 20th century, when the major source of funding for criminal helping organizations had shifted to government, management had largely become social service professionals from the ranks of college sociology departments.

Their influence had many disastrous effects within the work of criminal rehabilitation and all work with the marginal, as noted by Hendershott (2002):

> In defending the marginal or powerless, sociologists shifted the focus of deviance to those persons and groups in society with the power to propose definitions. Attention began to move from the criminal, the drug addict, the prostitute, the mentally ill and the homeless, to those who were seen to have branded them as deviant, or "caused" their deviance...a punitive criminal justice system that targeted the poor and oppressed was viewed as the cause of crime...

> Criminals were redefined as victims of an unfair economy that effectively locked them out of legitimate opportunities...Drug abuse was transformed from a moral and legal issue into a medical one. Drug abusers were then redefined as victims either of their own genes, or of an oppressive society that forced

them to take drugs in order to dull the pain of their rejection. (pp. 4-5)

Whatever success had been accomplished before the tenure of the sociologists—through the government sponsored Great Society programs developed and funded by President's Kennedy and Johnson—turned to dust during their thirty years of leadership. By the 21st century any program working with criminals that could point to a well-documented, rigorously evaluated and significant success were essentially non-existent.

However, sociology breaks down—in its defining of reality—as surely as in defining of deviancy, as it is merely that, a *definition* based on an ideology rather than truth, solid revealed truth—from before the foundation of the world.

105) For most traditional rehabilitation programs, the concept revolved around adding insult to injury. The initial injury, from the criminal's perspective, is the arrest, jail and prison confinement. The insult is presenting rudimentary behavioral norms—not even believed by the culture—in a sophomoric way to street-savvy people who are a captive audience. The criminals respond to evaluative surveys with how much they like the program, they are rehabilitated, and can I go home now? Starkly put, this is the state of too many traditional rehabilitation programs.

106) Recently however, returning to its roots, the nonprofit human service sector began government funding of faith-based organizations under the rubric of compassionate conservatism.

The history of this movement is described by Olasky (2000):

> The word *compassion* from the 1960's through the early 1990's was as much a code word for liberals as *family values* has become for conservatives. *Compassion* no longer conveyed what its literal dictionary definition states: compassion as "suffering with," reflecting the close personal tie of a caring individual and a person in distress....
>
> In the early 1980's Bob Woodson, head of the National Center for Neighborhood Enterprise, ...argued that small neighborhood groups could do a much better job of revitalizing urban communities than could the grand projects of the Great Society. He put together conferences of street gang members gone straight and of tenants who wanted to manage and eventually own their housing projects. (p.2, italics in original)

This is essentially the concept of subsidiarity in action, that those closest to the problem could best develop solutions to it.

However, as yet there isn't any evidence of much success with faith-based programs, according to recent meta-analysis conducted by the Washington State Institute of Public Policy (2006):

> The faith-based offender programs that have been evaluated to date do not significantly reduce recidivism. Rigorous evaluations of

faith-based programs are still relatively rare—we found only five thorough evaluations—and future studies may provide evidence of better outcomes. (p. 7)

That is also the case with faith-based efforts in a more focused way, that of faith-based job programs, noted by Kennedy & Bielfeld (2006):

In our study, we found no evidence to support the contention that faith-based contractors are more effective that secular providers. (p. 177)

I would contend this is more the result of faith-based efforts that are not sectarian, but are so generalized due to the legal barriers to conducting faith-based work, that they are essentially neutering their primary effectiveness benchmark, that of conversion.

107) The Holy See (1997), in expressing the principle of subsidiarity, also notes the often negative consequences—as were evident from the Great Society programs—that can arise from excessive state intervention:

Excessive intervention by the state can threaten personal freedom and initiative. The teaching of the Church has elaborated the principle of *subsidiarity,* according to which "a community of a higher order should not interfere in the internal life of a community of a lower order, depriving the latter of its function, but rather should support it in case of need and help to co-ordinate its activity with the activities of the rest of society, always with a view to the common good." (#1883, italics in original)

In seeking conversion from a criminal culture deeply valued by its members—particularly its leadership—it is imperative that this closeness govern action.

Within the mystery of the criminal culture, regardless of the vast amount of cultural material describing it allowing outsiders to believe they comprehend its internalities, the deepest markers for understanding are experiential, and it is only from that basis that cultural understanding can emerge.

Culture Only Criminals Understand

108) When the culture becomes criminalized, the only ones who understand it are the criminals.

Culture criminalized—as are modern cultural artifacts—is a milieu criminal's move confidently in. I am using artifact here in the organizational sense as developed by Schein (1997) to analyze organizational culture:

At the surface we have the level of *artifacts*, which includes all the phenomena that one sees, hears and feels when one encounters a new group with an unfamiliar culture. Artifacts would include the visible products of the group such as the architecture of its physical environment, its language, its technology and products, its artistic creations, and its style as embodied in clothing, manners of address, emotional displays, myths and stories... (p. 17)

109) A criminalized world is a world built upon traditional criminal phenomena of predatory acquisition, the untrammeled satisfying of sensual urge, and violence—real or threatened—as a major negotiating tool.

Some of the criminalization of culture in my time upon this earth, springs from those words and ideas flowing from the false sense of freedom and individuality surrounding the beat period—as shaped by Burroughs, Ginsburg and Kerouac, which laid the foundation for the 1960's—expressed primarily against the institution of the Catholic Church which, ironically, most strongly protects that freedom and individuality through its social teaching.

Kerouac, the major chronicler of this period, even naming it, realized at some level, perhaps from the deep well of his Catholicism, that what they were doing was evil, noted by Charters (1992):

[Kerouac's] *decision to become a writer was encouraged by Allen Ginsburg, Lucien Carr, and William Burroughs, but in the autobiographical novel* Vanity of Duluoz *(1968), which Kerouac wrote late in life about the period 1939-1946, he expressed reservations about his friends' wild behavior. In describing their association with criminals and drug dealers, and his own Benzedrine and alcohol addictions, he acknowledged that this "clique was the most evil and intelligent buncha bastards and shits in America but had to admire in my admiring youth."* (p. 8, italics in original)

110) Great joy was felt when the poem—censored as obscene—*Howl* by Allen Ginsberg, was smuggled into the nation's prisons, at the clear message that criminals were, after all, the "best minds of my generation".

As noted by Ginsberg's (1956) first line:

I saw the best minds of my generation destroyed by madness, starving hysterical naked, ragging themselves through the negro streets at dawn looking for an angry fix,
angelheaded hipsters burning for the ancient heavenly connection to the starry dynamo in the machinery of night, (p. 9)

In the dull and dreary cement encased confincs of prison, this was a revolutionary document and under no conditions would it have been allowed to be read openly by the criminals imprisoned there as anyone reading it could see what it glorified and ultimately portended.

We have gone so far beyond that attempt by society to censor material, that in today's world, Taylor (2001) can accurately note:

Today's children and youth routinely use the metaphors of prison life to portray their own lives outside of prison. (p. 18)

Part Three: Deep Knowledge Leadership

"A desire to work for the common good is not enough. The way to make this desire effective is to form competent men and women who can transmit to others the maturity which they themselves have achieved." (St. Josemaria Escriva, Conversations with St. Josemaria Escriva. p. 115))

Mapping the Terrain

111) Before venturing into the wasteland heed the guides who have returned.

T. E. Lawrence (2000): describes the outsider's attempt to be part of a mission of moment:

> A man who gives himself to be a possession of aliens leads a Yahoo life, having bartered his soul to a brute-master. He is not of them. He may stand against them, persuade himself of a mission, batter and twist them into something which they, of their own accord, would not have been. Then he is exploiting his old environment to press them out of theirs. Or, after my model, he may imitate them so well that they spuriously imitate him back again. Then he is giving away his own environment: pretending to

theirs; and pretences are hollow, worthless things. In neither case does he do a thing of himself, nor a thing so clean as to be his own (without thought of conversion), letting them take what action or reaction they please from the silent example. (p. 5)

112) In my previous book, Lukenbill (2006), I began the process of defining deep knowledge leadership:

Deep knowledge is the knowledge that comes from experience, is shaped through education, and informed by Catholic social teaching.

As I continued deepening my own knowledge around criminal justice issues, social teaching, higher education, and my consulting experience, it became clear the embrace of a deeper level of knowledge is required for effective work with criminal transformation, which ultimately requires dealing with the deepest part of a criminal's spiritual, emotional, and intellectual being.

Traditional books about working with people from life's margins often talk about how those comfortably situated in the center of the modern world can reach out to the marginal, and Kennedy (1997) offers this:

"Bridging the gap is not just giving food and lodging to those who are hungry and homeless and praying for them. It means eating with them, living with them, praying with them." (p. 7)

But that is not far or deep enough and I would end that sentence with these words: *and looking to them for leadership in solving the problems creating the gap needing bridging,* and as far as criminal transformation is concerned, from a Catholic perspective, *faith in doing* is not deep enough. What is required here is *faith in being.* (p. 41)

113) Deep knowledge about criminal transformation is knowledge deeply embedded within the transformed criminal through three benchmarks I have established based on my analysis of the time and processes needed to acquire and embrace it.

1) The searing of experience:

- Having been involved for ten years in the criminal world committing crimes for money,
- Having served five years in a maximum security federal or state prison,
- Being ten years out of prison, off parole, crime free, and helping the community.

2) The sharpening of education:

- Possessing a Master's degree,

- Belonging to criminal justice and nonprofit management related professional associations.
- A commitment to lifelong learning.

3) The harmonizing of spiritual growth:

- Being a leader of a community criminal transformation program,
- Being married in a strong and committed Catholic partnership,
- Being involved in extended self-study of Catholic social teaching with a basic knowledge of the key concepts.

114) Some reentry practitioners realize that involving former criminals in traditional rehabilitation work is valuable as Travis (2005) notes:

> The prison experience for some individuals results in an added obligation of citizenship; namely these ex-prisoners strive to work for criminal justice reform, to provide a helping hand to the next generation of returning prisoners, and to persuade young people to avoid involvement with crime. **The voices and contributions of these "wounded leaders" are undervalued societal assets. Our reentry policies should particularly celebrate those former prisoners who want to help others to successfully integrate.**

(p. 339 highlighting added)

This added involvement is an important part of what can be done along with the additional layers of knowledge that will allow these "wounded leaders" the wherewithal to run programs effectively.

115) Many criminals, after being released from prison, spending time on the outside, maybe gaining some college—but with no management experience, and little spiritual grounding—are inclined and fortunate enough to acquire funding for a criminal transformation program. However, due to their lack of management knowledge and spiritual grounding, are only able to manage it for a few years—even though perhaps very successfully—after which they become 'burnt-out' and leave the management of it to someone else who runs it into the ground.

This is a story replicated within the human service field in general, and with the depth of sorrow, anger, and pain accompanying working in the criminal transformative world specifically, you need tools of corresponding depth to survive the suffering and reach a level of sustainability to begin to realize the joy of this most rewarding work.

116) The most important tool needed is spiritual grounding and understanding the suffering you have brought upon others and yourself.

Time spent in prison and deep involvement in the criminal world, is time that ultimately causes deep suffering to the individual.

It does not matter that the pain of suffering arises from action you set into motion yourself or not, it is still pain.

It arises—the suffering prison causes—from action in the city of men, from action taken by the criminal in the city of men to survive, to survive in a city whose animating voice is to eat or be eaten.

It is your dignity that is scratched, clawed, and tore at, and it is this the criminal fights to protect, and it is the still, small voice of protection the Catholic Church has raised for centuries—to protect individual dignity no matter the action that individual has taken—which provides the only safe harbor, the only home, to the criminal transforming.

I believe that the criminal transforms—will only transform—to a higher truth than that of the criminal world and the Catholic Church is the truth that must be presented to the criminal for him to be able to make the transformation.

117) The truth from Jesus Christ was fought against from the beginning with the many heresies the early Church fathers had to address, through the split of the eastern churches and that of the protestants, continuing until the present now, when anyone who can find something in the bible they feel they can claim as their particular truth, forms another religious community around it.

It is truly the tower of Babel and the preying wolves spoken of, and the ongoing work of the prince of this world to destroy the truth throughout history, but the Church stands as Christ foretold and the gates of hell have not prevailed against her.

118) Maritain (2001) describes an aspect of deep knowledge the fathers of the Church understood:

> The notion of knowledge through connaturality—that is, of a kind of knowledge which is produced in the intellect but not by virtue of conceptual connections and by way of demonstration—seems to me to be of particular importance, both because of the considerable part played by this kind of knowledge in human existence, and because it obliges us to realize in a deeper manner the *analogous* character of the concept of knowledge....

> St. Thomas explains in this way the differences between the knowledge of divine reality acquired by theology and the knowledge of divine reality acquired by mystical experience. For the spiritual man, he says, knows divine things through inclination or connaturality, **not only because he has learned them, but, as the Pseudo-Dionysius put it, because he suffers them.** (pp. 13-15 italics in original, highlighting added)

This analogousness is crucial, in that without the balance of the criminal experiential knowledge with the criminal justice, organizational, academic, and social teaching knowledge, the ability to penetrate the often deceptive signals surrounding rehabilitative action in the carceral/criminal world will be virtually nil; explaining the failure of the traditional rehabilitative practitioner over these past several decades.

The criminal, having transformed the pain of his suffering into the power of teaching, and having transformed his love of the transitory truth of the world—the foundation stones of criminal world knowledge—into the virtuous ladder of communal living, with deep refreshment at the sacrificial table of the Mass, will embody the deep knowledge his experience, faith, and learning shapes, with a fierce conviction.

Guiding Criminal Justice Principles

119) The deep knowledge leader will need to adopt principles of criminal justice which he has learned from experience and education which resonate with reality.

The formal foundation of Judeo-Christian criminal justice principles was established in Exodus 20:22 to 23:20, the *Book of the Covenant.*

It is described by Navarre (1999):

This collection of laws is usually described as the "Book of the Covenant" on account of what is said in 24:7, or the "Code of the Covenant", because many of these laws are similar to those to be found in legal codes of Semitic peoples, such as the Sumerian code of Ur-Nammu (c. 2050 BC), that of Esnunna (c. 1950 BC), that of Lipit-Istar (c. 1850 BC) and (the most famous) code of Hammurabi (c. 1700 BC), which is conserved on a dioritic stone in the Louvre Museum, Paris.

The laws collected here probably existed earlier in a similar or even identical wording, but by being inserted into the Book of the Covenant in the context of the events of Sinai they acquire extra weight and authority. They become as it were the "basic laws" of the people, ratified by God himself. (p. 331)

For the deep knowledge leader working in the United States, these criminal justice principles will help guide our work.

1) Broken windows policing works.

120) Allowing even the minor violation of a broken window in an area helps create the impression of an environment where law and order does not prevail and where crime flourishes. Responding quickly and efficiently to all crimes, regardless of the perceived state of seriousness or other local community concerns, is the foundation of good police work.

The Vatican Catechism (2007) teaches:

2266 The State's effort to contain the spread of behaviors injurious to human rights and the fundamental rules of civil

111

coexistence corresponds to the requirement of watching over the common good.

2) The response to crime should be timely, balanced, and just.

121) When justice is for sale, either through wealth, influence, or ideology, a fertile soil is created from which crime grows. The training and education of professionals in the criminal justice system is built on a foundation of traditional and well-reasoned concepts of justice and it needs continual reinforcement to remain an effective response to crime.

> You shall do no injustice in judgment; you shall not be partial to the poor or defer to the great, but in righteousness shall you judge your neighbor. (Leviticus 19:15)

3) Prison is the most appropriate criminal sanction to protect society and punish the criminal, while allowing the opportunity for criminal reformation.

122) Prison is an effective sanction for crime which has been used by human beings since ancient times. It serves to protect the public from predatory crime, acts as a deterrence and as incapacitation, and allows the penitential criminal the opportunity—while removed from the community—to reflect upon and correct his criminal behavior.

From the U. S. Bishops (2006):

> **468.** A punishment imposed by legitimate public authority has the aim of redressing the disorder introduced by the offense, of defending public order and people's safety, and contributing to the correction of the guilty party. *Compendium: Catechism of the Catholic Church* (2006) (p. 137)

4) Capital punishment is an appropriate response to the criminal evil of murder, rape and pedophilia.

123) Capital punishment is often the only effective social method available to protect the innocent and applied with dispatch after legal review of the crimes charged and determining the fitness of its application, should be considered an appropriate sentence for murderers, rapists and pedophiles; who, knowing the time of their death, are able, with certainty of their remaining time to do so, seek God's forgiveness.

Correctional professionals realize that if a pedophile is placed into a maximum security prison, where the population is primarily professional criminals, he will soon be killed, which poses an interesting question: "Why would the criminal respond more aggressively to the abuse of a child than the non-criminal?"

However, five states, as of May 2008, have approved the use of capital punishment in child rape cases; Louisiana, Montana, Oklahoma, South Carolina, and Texas.

From the Vatican Catechism (2007):

> **2267** The traditional teaching of the Church does not exclude, presupposing full ascertainment of the identity and responsibility of the offender, recourse to the death penalty, when this is the only practicable way to defend the lives of human beings effectively against the aggressor.

From the Summa Theologia (1920)

> According to the order of His wisdom, God sometimes slays sinners forthwith in order to deliver the good, whereas sometimes He allows them time to repent, according as He knows what is expedient for His elect. Thus also does human justice imitate according to its powers; for it puts to death those who are dangerous to others, while it allows time for repentance to those who sin without grievously harming others...
>
> When, however, they fall into very great wickedness, and become incurable, we ought no longer to show them friendliness. It is for this reason that both Divine and human laws command such like sinners to be put to death, because there is greater likelihood of their harming others than of their mending their ways. Nevertheless the judge puts this

into effect, not out of hatred for the sinners, but out of the love of charity, by reason of which he prefers the public good to the life of the individual. Moreover the death inflicted by the judge profits the sinner, if he be converted, unto the expiation of his crime; and, if he be not converted, it profits so as to put an end to the sin, because the sinner is thus deprived of the power to sin any more. (St. Thomas Aquinas, II-II, Ques. 25, Article 6, reply to objection 2.)

5) Repentant criminals deserve a second chance.

124) Excepting those cases of serious predatory behavior deserving the death penalty or natural life in prison, repentant criminals, once they have clearly shown—over a ten year period after being released from criminal justice supervision—that they have transformed their life by becoming a productive member of their family, their church, their work, and their community, should be allowed to apply for a complete pardon in a simple straightforward process.

From Caesar forgiveness may be sought but is rarely given, but from God forgiveness is always given. The Vatican Catechism teaches:

982 There is no offense, however serious, that the Church cannot forgive. There is no one, however wicked and guilty, who may not confidently hope for forgiveness, provided his repentance is honest. Christe who died for all men desires that in his Church the gates of forgiveness should always be open to anyone who turns away from sin.

6) It takes a reformed criminal to reform criminals.

125) For generations the ability of non-criminals—even those with the highest professional and academic credentials—to effectively rehabilitate criminals has proven, based on sound evaluations, to be virtually non-existent. Recruiting reformed criminals who have, through education, training, and the development of a deep knowledge leadership approach to criminal transformation, may well succeed where others have failed. Considering the current recidivism rate of 70%, and with the consensus that peer-based help does, at the very least, attract those who want help to transformative programs, it is time to try this approach in a substantial enough way, over time and properly evaluated, to discover if we can rely on it as a valuable tool for large-scale implementation.

As I wrote in an earlier book, Lukenbill (2006):

> Transformed criminals with advanced degrees and Catholic social teaching knowledge—I describe as deep knowledge leaders—working through grassroots community organizations, can help reverse the long-term failure of criminal

rehabilitation programs, as they possess the elemental experiential knowledge of the criminal world allowing them, and them only, the authentic access to criminals long denied the social work professional. (p. 9)

7) In the work of criminal reformation, it is vital to keep in mind that the criminal—not society, capitalism, or the criminal justice system—is the problem.

126) Some criminal justice advocates take the position that among the people connected with the carceral world, the good guys are the criminals; and the police, district attorneys, prison guards, and the legislators who support stringent criminal sanctions, are the bad guys.

This is the absolutely wrong position, for in virtually any carceral population in America it is the criminals who are the indisputable bad guys, while the good guys are the ones protecting the public from the depredations of criminals. Those who parlay the myths of Hollywood or Marxism into an intellectual stance that fails to understand this basic fact, does everyone a disservice in particular the penitential criminal—who may find little reason for proper expiation within a culture defining criminality as somehow admirable.

Conclusion

127) Like many fields, criminal justice often benefits from or is hurt by ideas that take hold of an influential group able to create foundational ideology from which taboos against opposing ideas can be created; but in the midst of these philosophical and sociological meanderings, the conclusions from one of the seminal thinkers in current crime and public policy remain valid:

> Rehabilitation has not yet been shown to be a promising method for dealing with serious offenders, broad-gauge investments in social progress have little near-term effect on crime rates, punishment is not an unworthy objective for the criminal justice system of a free and liberal society to pursue, the evidence supports (though cannot conclusively prove) the view that deterrence and incapacitation work, and new crime-control techniques ought to be tried in a frankly experimental manner with a heavy emphasis on objective evaluation.

> **—James Q. Wilson (1975)** *Thinking About Crime* **(Rev. Ed. 1983) p. 5—**

Sherpas', Apostles & Forbidden Knowledge

128) Climbing Mount Everest with its own climate, trails, geography, and general conditions unlike any other place, requires knowledgeable guides for even the most experienced climbers to find success and eventually stand at its peak.

The Sherpa guides live on the mountain and call the Himalayas home. They are the only people with the life experience so vital to really *knowing* the mountain, and it is only in *knowing it* that one can traverse it.

Without having been on Everest it's impossible to explain the conditions to an outsider, as they do not match anything experienced in any of earth's other regions.

It is a world unto itself, whose environment has been built over eons of weather shaping rocks, animals shaping trails, and the often futile efforts by humans, except for the Sherpas, of trying to conquer it.

The Sherpa's know that you really don't conquer Everest; you learn to live with it long enough to survive the climb up it.

129) This is analogous to the criminal world. This is what it is like to the outsider who attempts to traverse it and conquer it, to find among its ancient trails the secrets to sampling and mastering its wiles and treasures long enough to discover their meaninglessness against the greater treasure of a truth bringing peace and harmony instead of the violence and chaos the criminal city visits upon its sojourners.

The transformed criminal is the Sherpa guide, the only one who can lead the sojourning penitential criminal to the top of the mountain of reformation.

130) In his encyclical *Quadragesimo Anno* (1931) Pope Pius XI teaches us, in speaking of the unions and their impact upon the state of affairs in the modern world, says, to let the workers be the apostles—the Sherpa Guides—to the workers:

141. The present state of affairs, Venerable Brethren, clearly indicates the way in which We ought to proceed. For We are now confronted, as more than once before in the history of the Church, with a world that in large part has almost fallen back into paganism. That these whole classes of men may be brought back to Christ Whom they have denied, we must recruit and train from among them, themselves, auxiliary soldiers of the Church who know them well and their minds and wishes, and can reach their hearts with a tender brotherly love. **The first and immediate apostles to the workers ought to be workers; the apostles to those who follow industry and trade ought to be from among them themselves.** (highlighting added)

131) In many ways, deep knowledge would also fit within the category of forbidden knowledge as illustrated by Shattuck (1996):

During the three hundred years since the Enlightenment, we have made life difficult for ourselves precisely in the domains of knowledge and truth. Having to a large extent dismissed any faith in revealed or absolute knowledge, how can we distinguish the true from the untrue? And while we seek empirical or pragmatic means to do so, another question, both larger and more precise, looms before us. Can we decide if there are any forms of knowledge, true or untrue, that for some reason *we should not know?* (p. 6)

And yes, in some ways, the deep knowledge of which I speak is knowledge we should not know, and in a better world Cain has not marked with his crime, perhaps it would not.

132) Criminals know that much of crime is enjoyable and rewarding, yet the traditional rehabilitative practitioner often focuses on only its negatives in an effort to make its pursuit less desirable, especially to youth.

This tendency creates great difficulty for those same practitioners as the criminals they are trying to rehabilitate don't have faith in their ability "to distinguish between the true and untrue" so why would they be believed about anything?

The youth they are trying to keep from a life of crime, once discovering for themselves how rewarding and pleasurable many aspects of crime can be, come to the same conclusion and disregard their entreaties.

Criminals Working With Criminals

133) Former criminals who have redeemed themselves working with other criminals to help them find the same path of redemption, is not a new concept, but what is new is the understanding that it cannot be merely the experience of the criminal that is valuable, but the academic, organizational, and spiritual knowledge he can obtain that will create a sustainable transformative organization.

The story of criminal-run organizations working in the area of prisoner reentry is long and deep and almost all of the stories have ended in failure.

Those that appear to have succeeded are residential-based programs that accept relatively few new people, who they screen well, and have not really been replicable; but without rigorous evaluations conducted by an independent evaluator and using a control group, it is impossible to determine their real success.

If we can accept these first three steps then the fourth seems axiomatic: 1) that criminal and carceral involvement is a valuable experiential knowledge base; and 2) that personal transformation through education and spiritual development may prove valuable in developing criminal transformative programs; while 3) advanced education and training in organizational management and Catholic social teaching will enable one to manage and sustain effective programs; then 4) it would be of great value for government to fund pilot programs.

134) One of the great difficulties with those approaching criminal transformation from the traditional rehabilitative stance—usually either a sociological or psychological perspective—is that there is no absoluteness, no absolute good or bad; so why rehabilitate from criminal world success, and so we are back in the relativism of the city of men, when what is needed is the clarity of the absolute City of God.

Many agree with Skotnicki (2002), who notes;

The model of criminal justice that is gaining swift ascent has simply absented itself from the moral question altogether in favor of isolating, monitoring, and recycling a perpetual class of offenders. This is the real demon that needs to be named and confronted. (p. 156)

In some sense, with the recent emphasis being shown in restoring rehabilitation into corrections—California even renamed its agency Department of Corrections and Rehabilitation—this has been modified. However, the core carceral and criminal world population still encompasses this perpetual class which continually and more deeply, is reshaping the criminal world territory, calling for leadership being sought from them, who are the only resource able to reach them in any substantive and transformative way.

135) Transformed criminals working with criminals will need to be contemplative and marital, using tools like the Spiritual Exercises of St. Ignatius, used for centuries to good effect by the Jesuits, once known as the shock troops of the Catholic empire.

The transformative power of their use is noted by Adam (1935):

> Karl Ludwig Schleich, late Professor of Surgery in Berlin, has some remarkable words about the "Spiritual Exercises" of St. Ignatius of Loyola. "I am profoundly convinced," he writes "and can therefore say

it quite confidently, that with these exercises and these rules in his hand a man might reform all our asylums, and prevent at least two-thirds of their inmates from ever entering them."(p. 235)

They will need to infuse their spirits with the truth of the Church to the level at which they can follow not only the Spiritual Exercises of St. Ignatius, but his Rules for Thinking With the Church, noted by Puhl (1951):

> 365. 13. If we wish to proceed securely in all things, we must hold fast to the following principle: What seems to me white, I will believe black if the hierarchical Church so defines. For I must be convinced that in Christ our Lord, the bridegroom, and in His spouse the Church, only one Spirit holds sway, which governs and rules for the salvation of souls. For it is by the same Spirit and Lord who gave the Ten Commandments that our holy Mother church is ruled and governed. (p. 160)

They will need to—not only think martially—but be valiant and fond of fighting verbally and not fearful of fighting physically, which usually comes with the experience of surviving in a maximum security prison.

They need to think of themselves, as did the early Jesuits, as those shock troops venturing into areas rarely entered in the way they will now be entering.

136) We have, from the early Church, an important message of the importance of shock troops who can go where others cannot, noted by Chautard (1946)

> It is very certain that the primitive Church, as we have already hinted, knew how to organize magnificent and numerous shock troops, in the midst of the faithful, and their virtues both struck the pagans with astonishment and excited the admiration of honest souls, even those most prejudiced against Christianity by their principles, their traditions, and their social background. Conversions were the result, even in circles to which no priest had access. (p. 163)

137) Jacques Maritain and his wife Raissa, formed one of the most devout and influential contemplative and martial couples in Catholic history, as noted by Barre (2005):

> They [Jacques and Raissa] fell madly in love, married, and after making a vow to commit suicide together if they found no satisfactory reason for existence, converted to Catholicism in 1906. They set forth, at first hesitatingly, on a long difficult, and fruitful crusade to restore the philosophy of Thomas Aquinas to its true place of honor, to support and encourage the works of contemporary artists and musicians in a Christian and truly humanistic culture, to defend democratic institutions and human rights

against the onslaughts of totalitarianism, to reconcile democracy with the political traditions of the Catholic Church and help prepare that Church for the reforms of the Second Vatican Council, and all the while leading together, and quite secretly, a life of intense prayer and contemplation.
(pp. xi-xii)

Their insistence on infusing their daily life with contemplation and prayer was the strength and clarity which led them to exert such tremendous influence on the Catholic and political world of the early 20th Century.

This contemplative and martial path—necessary to work effectively in our world where information and communications access us with astonishing speed—is vital to remain centered. In the work of criminal transformation the spiritual path is core, but along with it is the martial spirit resonating throughout the history of America and embraced by its most effective military leaders.

138) Also centrally important is to embrace the vision of the Church Triumphant and Militant; that great assemblage, stretching out through history and time, of the great saints, the archangels leading the heavenly hosts, the knights of times past, and the knights and saints of today, wielding swords of spirit, light shimmering from their blades; their banners of the Word carried as they advance against the eternal enemy, the prince of this world, who has been in a battling retreat since being banished from Heaven by St. Michael.

There are orders within the Church which incorporate this spirit; in many ways so like the ancient priests of the true faith, clothed in priestly garb always, resolute in their devotion and union to Holy Mother Church, and to the Rock of Peter, upon whom the gates of hell never have and never will prevail.

139) For most people, working in the field of the professional criminal is prohibitively dangerous work —perhaps why the professional criminal justice practitioner has largely retreated from direct contact with it.

For the transformed criminal it is still dangerous, though with a strong grounding in the virtually impenetrable armor of daily mass, daily rosary, morning and evening prayers, daily reflections, mortification, and regular spiritual direction from a priest; it will be the work of the highest spiritual order, work of great apostolate reward and deep personal joy, the work of a lifetime, work for an eternity of lifetimes.

Part Four: Teaching Communal Reentry

670 *When the children of God act in their apostolate, they have to be like those great lighting systems which fill the world with light, but the lamp is not seen.* (St. Josemaria Escriva, *The Forge*)

The Papal Teaching

140) The Church, existing as a universal entity within the Kingdom of God, proclaims the essence of the apostolate to deep knowledge leaders, as noted by Lubac (1982):

> If therefore, the Church is mother, each Christian also is or should be a mother. In his place, according to his own vocation, in union with all the others, he participates in the maternal function of the Church. (p. 79)

In this Mother Church, founded before time, and existing as an earthly institution for over two thousand years and comprising today over one billion souls, it is vital that there be one teaching voice of clarity, strength, and vision from which the deep knowledge leader can continually refresh himself at the well of Catholic learning for the arduous task ahead.

That teaching voice is Peter. It is to Peter Christ entrusted the Church and it is from Peter that we seek the meaning of the work of the earthly Church, clarification of the eternal Gospel, education about the social teaching, and guidance for our apostolate.

141) The major source for the teachings of Peter are the papal encyclicals and studying them is a necessary aspect of educating ourselves about the social teaching.

In this digital age, access to the Vatican is easily obtained 24/7 and when studying the words of Peter, it is crucial to read the Vatican translations directly from the Vatican website.

I first discovered the encyclicals during my studies on my way into the Church as it soon became clear that I needed to find a place, in addition to the Catechism, for authoritative teaching; and so I found the papal encyclicals, the great storehouse of the Church, where all of the crystallized knowledge of her great thinkers finds their home.

The papal encyclicals—drawing from scripture and the Church fathers—really form the interpretive bedrock of the social teaching, from those written by Leo XIII to Pope Benedict XVI.

142) Reading the encyclicals is difficult to begin with, but once you understand the Vatican's need to write universally for the Church whose audience is truly *universal,* the preciseness and deep beauty of the language starts to resonate within you.

My practice is to download the encyclical I am studying to my computer, read a few pages or less, highlight and make notes in brackets, and mark where I left off to begin when I come back to it.

For many months during RCIA I studied this way every morning and it was a wonderful entrance to the blessed knowledge of Peter, who truly is our pastor.

As Pope Benedict XVI (2005), in his first encyclical *Deus Caritas Est*, teaches:

> **27.** It must be admitted that the Church's leadership was slow to realize that the issue of the just structuring of society needed to be approached in a new way. There were some pioneers, such as Bishop Kettler of Mainz (died 1877), and concrete needs were met by a growing number of groups, associations, leagues, federations and, in particular, by the new religious orders founded in the nineteenth century to combat poverty, disease and the need for better education. In 1891, the papal magisterium intervened with the Encyclical *Rerum Novarum* of Leo XIII. This was followed in 1931 by Pius XI's Encyclical *Quadragesimo Anno*. In 1961 Blessed John XXIII published the Encyclical *Mater et Magistra*, while Paul VI, in the Encyclical *Populorum Progressio* (1967) and in the Apostolic Letter *Octogesima Adveniens* (1971), insistently addressed the social problem, which had meanwhile become especially acute in Latin America. My great predecessor John Paul II left us a trilogy of social Encyclicals: *Laborem Exercens* (1981), *Sollicitudo Rei*

Socialis (1987) and finally *Centesimus Annus* (1991). Faced with new situations and issues, Catholic social teaching thus gradually developed, and has now found a comprehensive presentation in the *Compendium of the Social Doctrine of the Church* published in 2004 by the Pontifical Council *Iustitia et Pax*. Marxism had seen world revolution and its preliminaries as the panacea for the social problem: revolution and the subsequent collectivization of the means of production, so it was claimed, would immediately change things for the better. This illusion has vanished. In today's complex situation, not least because of the growth of a globalized economy, the Church's social doctrine has become a set of fundamental guidelines offering approaches that are valid even beyond the confines of the Church: in the face of ongoing development these guidelines need to be addressed in the context of dialogue with all those seriously concerned for humanity and for the world in which we live." (#27)

143) The Church, led by the office of Peter, the Bishop of Rome, which has been occupied by many men, some fallible, many saints, but all, in their own way kept the Barque of Peter intact as the vessel of the Church, always moving on its eternal voyage, always suffering through history and time, as noted by Pope Benedict XVI (2006):

The Church—and in her, Christ—still suffers today. In her Christ is again and again taunted and slapped; again and again an effort is made to remove him from the world. Again and again the little barque of the Church is ripped apart by the winds of ideologies, whose waters seep into her and seem to condemn her to sink. Yet, precisely in the suffering Church, Christ is victorious.

In spite of all, faith in him acquires ever new strength. The Lord also commands the waters today and shows that he is Lord of the elements. He stays in his barque, in the little boat of the Church. (n.p. June 29, 2006)

While it is important to study the teaching of all who have been pope, it is also most crucial to keep up with Peter's weekly teaching with *L' Osservatore Romano*, the official newspaper of the Holy See, which you can subscribe to through the Cathedral Foundation in Baltimore, and the daily teaching from the *Vatican Information Service* will deliver daily news about Peter's work, right to your email box.

Communal Reentry

144) The central concept animating successful communal reentry is the respect and maintenance of human dignity, one realized many years ago by a reformed criminal writing about criminals. Irwin (1970) writes:

[F]rom the standpoint of the felon a successful postprison life is more than merely staying out of prison. From the criminal ex-convict perspective it must contain other attributes, mainly it must be dignified. This is not generally understood by correctional people whose ideas on success are dominated by narrow and unrealistic conceptions of nonrecidivism and reformation. Importantly, because of their failure to recognize the felon's viewpoint, his aspirations, his conceptions of respect and dignity, or his foibles, they leave him to travel the difficult route away from the prison without guidance or assistance; in fact, with considerable hindrance, and with few avenues out of a criminal life acceptable both to him and his former keepers. (p. 204)

Traditional reentry programs fail to recognize this need for dignity, relying instead on a deviant model of criminality—creating hindrances—virtually guaranteeing non-acceptance by the criminal, even if he is seeking to build a different life.

Communal reentry is into the community of the Catholic Church, accepting and living its sacraments, growing in understanding of its social teaching, working through the personal apostolate of a transformed criminal—a deep knowledge leader and wise elder—and from this foundation, he is helping a friend, a fellow sojourner on the journey to Rome.

145) St. Paul, writing from prison in Rome in the winter of 63, to the Ephesians, teaches us:

> 19) So then you are no longer strangers and sojourners, but you are fellow citizens with the saints and members of the household of God, 20) built upon the foundation of the apostles and prophets, Christ Jesus himself being the cornerstone, 21) in whom the whole structure is joined together and grows into a holy temple in the Lord; 22) in whom you also are built into it for a dwelling place of God in the Spirit. (Ephesians 2:19-22)

Along with the bonds of sacramental marriage and the children from that marriage, this is the first community and for most transformed criminals, perhaps the last.

This community, this primary community of the transformed criminal, is the communion of saints—the Church Triumphant—and his true pastor is Peter, whose homilies he reads daily, and his local parish is any welcoming building where he attends Mass and receives Christ, all part of the true community we are blessed to be part of, the Kingdom of God.

146) The transformation from the criminal world to the Catholic communal world—the Kingdom of God—is a process of traversing through three spiritual stages.

The first stage is the spiritual understanding that the truths being followed to maintain status in the criminal world are inferior, in an objective sense, from those governing the communal world.

This stage requires intense study—academic and theological—to reach an initial concluding step that God exists.

The second stage is a study of the communal world, learning about the culture and ways of living. This is primarily an experiential learning process of being involved with parish life as a sacramental Catholic.

The third stage is acceptance of an apostolate, which for a transformed criminal can be none other than that of helping other criminals who are lost find their way home to Rome.

Being a professional criminal is a committed life only fully exorcised through use of the goodness gifted by God's grace resulting from the transformation from the evil of its wrongful living.

147) Saint Maria Faustine Kowalska (2007) writes of the three degrees of spiritual growth:

> The priest spoke these profound words to me, "There are three degrees in the accomplishment of God's will: in the first, the soul carries out all rules and statues pertaining to external observance; in the second degree, the soul accepts interior inspirations and carries them out faithfully; in the third degree, the soul, abandoned to the will of God, allows Him to dispose of it freely, and God does with it as He pleases, and it is a docile tool in His hands."
> (pp. 195-196)

148) In the Beatitudes opening the Sermon on the Mount, Christ begins by saying: "Blessed are the poor in spirit, for theirs is the kingdom of heaven." (Matthew 5: 3), and it is here that the soul abandoned to God, knowing that all that comes, comes from God; completely trusting, as a little child, that God will do with him as he needs to be done with according to his highest nature, and that whatever happens, all will be well.

149) The potency of the confessional booth, alone with the priest, allows the flowering and deepening of guilt, even though forgiveness of sin is given with penance, the guilt in the sinner remains a strong spur to conscience acting on him in the future.

This single relationship, of one human to another is continued in the reentry program model Lampstand uses for the same purpose.

The difficulty with the group model, used in most of the work with criminals, is that it removes guilt rather than deepening it, thus also removing the spur to conscience needed for strength in the future.

As the wrongs committed are expressed within the group, with the promise to do better, the group forgives but without the professional and spiritual insight and expertise of the Catholic priest, and the message received is that it is okay to fall down, you are expected to fail, everyone does.

Though this therapeutic community approach appears to be the practice of much group oriented work with the alcoholic/addict/criminal population, and may even result in some benefit, the expectation of failure can be a fatal practice for criminals and their victims.

The transformative work occurs in the relationship of one to one, human to human, human to God.

The Kingdom of God

150) The Church, the repository of revealed truth, grows through the communion of each Catholic embracing that truth, taking in that Word of truth from Jesus Christ, learning from its shaping and exposition through the centuries by the saints of the Church, and from the work of each apostolate.

Working through the apostolate, helping birth the transformation of criminals, and they, having been reborn in the Church, add to the teaching of the word.

It is within the Kingdom of God that two of the ancient covenants with God are embraced, the Old Covenant with the Jews, to prepare the way, to create the conditions among a people for the new, and the New Covenant with everyone.

The Kingdom of God is a universal kingdom of the spirit and its external organizational structure is the Catholic Church.

Tanquerey (2000) notes:

a) The central idea of Christ's teaching as recorded by the Synoptics is that of the *Kingdom of God*...It is presented under a threefold form: 1) At times it is the Kingdom of Heaven, or the place reserved for the Elect: "Come, ye blessed of my Father, possess you the kingdom prepared for you

from the foundation of the world." (Mat. 25:34). 2) At other times it is the *interior* kingdom as already established upon earth, that is to say, grace, friendship, sonship bestowed by God and received by men of good-will. 3) Lastly, it is the *external* kingdom which God establishes in order to perpetuate His work in the world. **b)** These three forms constitute but one and the same kingdom; for the visible Church was founded only to enable the interior kingdom to expand peacefully, and the latter is, so to speak, the sum-total of the conditions that open to us the kingdom of heaven.
(p. Appendices 1*, italics in the original)

And the Holy See (1997), in the Catechism, notes:

The proclamation of the Kingdom of God

543 *Everyone* is called to enter the kingdom. First announced to the children of Israel, this messianic kingdom is intended to accept men of all nations. To enter it, one must first accept Jesus' word:

> The world of the Lord is compared to a seed which is sown in a field; those who hear it with faith and are numbered among the little flock of Christ have truly received the kingdom. Then, by its own power, the

seed sprouts and grows until the harvest.

544 The kingdom belongs *to the poor and lowly*, which means those who have accepted it with humble hearts. ...

545 Jesus invites *sinners* to the table of the kingdom: "I came not to call the righteous, but sinners."... (p. 139)

Pope Benedict XVI (2007) teaches us:

When Jesus speaks of the Kingdom of God, he is quite simply proclaiming God and proclaiming him to be the living God, who is able to act concretely in the world and in history and is even now so acting. He is telling us: "God exists" and "God is really God," which means that he holds in his hands the threads of the world. (pp. 53-54)

The Kingdom of God is the kingdom where all can live, finding eternal life, most importantly the penitential criminal, whose sin is greatest and whom Christ has called before all others, for did not He take the good thief Dismas with him to heaven, thereby creating the first canonized saint of the Church.

Conclusion

Deep calls to deep at the thunder of thy cataracts; all thy waves and thy billows have gone over me. (Ps. 42:7)

151) This book has been about the strategy of using reformed criminals to develop and manage criminal transformative efforts, but while I presuppose no absolute success in those efforts, I would anticipate a substantial increase in the current 30% success rate of reentry if the fullness of the ideas being expressed here are adopted and supported by government—through grants for programs and by including transformed criminals working in the nonprofit sector within the benefits of the College Cost Reduction and Access Act of 2007 which provides loan forgiveness after ten years of public service—and the Catholic Church who could be the first funder of demonstration programs in California, New York, and Florida.

152) The Catholic Church has traditionally operated from three models of their involvement in the world, from the foundation of their social teaching, as noted by Merkle (2004):

> The first is an educational-cultural model...emphasizes actions of the Church that communicate and develop a Catholic moral vision, values, sense of the common good, and a critical reflection on culture...A second model is the legislative-policy model.

Here the Church engages in the public life of society, entering into the civic process by which policy and legislation are formed....A third model is the prophetic-witness model. Here the Church as a whole or a community from within, acts as a clear counterpoint, to existing societal vision and policies.
(pp. 178-179)

Beginning to implement the ideas in this book would touch on all three of these models. In the first model; helping to reshape the current—almost purely punitive social handling of criminals—towards the traditional Catholic redemptive and forgiveness model, based on the ultimate power God has for forgiveness and transformation when the human heart reaches truly out for that grace.

In the second model; it will take legislation to enact approval for rehabilitative programs developed and managed by transformed criminals, and the process of public education around the issues involved will be a steep one.

In the third model; the prophetic-witness comes from the transformed criminals themselves, who once lost have been found, and return to the communal world as the prodigal son with an ability to reach other criminals at a deeper and more truthful level than anyone else has yet been able to do so.

153) Criminal transformative efforts rely first of all on the truthfulness of the criminal to the transformative agent, and yet still, former criminals are almost as susceptible as being lied to, and accepting the lies, as most other transformative practitioners.

The success difference might be slight in the beginning, so instead of seven of every ten returning to prison under the current regime, maybe that could be lowered to four of ten and perhaps even three of ten, (turning the current statistics of a 70% recidivist rate around to one of 30%) bringing us closer to the 19th century reported recidivist rate—though evaluation of individual programs was rudimentary at best— when most American criminal justice work was in the hands of the religious, of one of ten, noted by Skotnicki (2000):

> The central coordinates of the separate and silent systems, silence, work, and moral/religious training, were not found to be ineffective as formal guiding principles...Despite the fact that the statistical methods utilized to determine the effects of the penitentiary discipline on recidivism often missed reconvictions in other states, were certainly tinged with ideological bias, and cannot be necessarily equated with penal methods, it would be a mistake to ignore their findings out of hand. The chaplains who conducted them were not always blind supporters of the administration. History provides clear evidence that they were willing, to a significant degree, to critique institutional practices. Still, their data concerning recidivism was most favorable. Prior to the

Civil War, the rates of reconviction were consistently less than 10%, with the data from the Eastern Penitentiary being the lowest. (p. 145)

154) Criminals are neither born criminal, though often born into a criminal world, nor made so by society—though in following the innate urge to seek truth may happen upon the truth of the world and the criminal city—which often becomes in its embracing and living, criminal.

Criminals are like all of us, children of God, but they have become lost—are lost so much deeper than most. Some so far they should never again be allowed intercourse with other humans, remaining forever in solitary confinement or subject to the imposition of the death penalty. Some so far they should never again be allowed physical freedom and spend the rest of their natural life in prison. Some are lost only as far as still having a possibility of social intercourse and personal freedom, and for some who have been lost and are now found, even a hope of a lifetime of penitential contribution through the way of the apostolate.

Given what I know of the capabilities and passion former criminals would be bringing to the transformative work, that does not seem far-fetched at all. It is surely a restorative vision to work towards.

And perhaps Christ, in his original gesture of taking with him from Calvary, Dismas the criminal, is expressing his will in a way perhaps long hidden from us in its fullest meaning.

155) Miller (2007) notes the potency of the original gesture, in the expression of Christ's will for the maleness of the priesthood:

> The Church is bound to follow an original gesture of Christ when he established the sacrament of Holy Orders. This is at once a Christological and an ecclesiological issue. When Christ called only men to the company of the Twelve, we are confronted by the will of Christ himself. (n.p.)

This thought deepens Christ's teaching, reinforced by the Church for so many generations, what he said at the beginning of his ministry:

> Those who are well have no need of a physician, but those who are sick; I came not to call the righteous, but sinners. (Mark 2:17)

156) Within the Kingdom of God, the formerly lost, the criminals first among them, marked our future.

St. Mary Magdalene, the former prostitute, was the first criminal to see Christ resurrected. St. Dismas, the former thief, was the first criminal to become a saint of the Church built on Peter. St. Callistus, the former thief, was the first criminal to become Peter.

Christ chose us, and we are perhaps the only ones—we transformed criminals who are Catholics—who can begin to empty the prisons and help the prodigal son return home.

The truth of Christ within the Church founded on the rock of Peter, prevailing over the gates of hell for these two thousand years, is the only truth trumping the truth of this world.

Only Christ defeats Satan, crushing his evil beneath his feet, casting him evermore into darkness; and only we are blessed and armed as spiritual warriors carrying the sword of the social teaching, refined in the blazing sensual fires of the criminal city whose glittering dust we have shaken from our feet, fashioned and blessed by the rites and sacraments of Mother Church, guided by Peter and Christ, able to venture into the deepest darkness here on earth to rescue the souls still lost there.

Only we few.

For all those criminals who studied deep things with me in the prisons, take care.

References

Adam, K. (1935). *The spirit of Catholicism* (Rev. Ed.). New York: The Macmillan Company.

Alighieri, D. (2002) *The inferno* (A. Esolen, Trans.). New York: The Modern Library.

Augustine, St. (1993 [426]). *The city of God*. New York: Modern Library.

Barre, J.L. (2005). *Jacques & Raissa Maritain: Beggars for heaven*. Norte Dame, Indiana: University of Norte Dame Press.

Beaumont, G. & Tocqueville, A. (*1833*-1964). *On the penitentiary system in the United States and its application in France*. Carbondale, Illinois: Southern Illinois University Press.

Beirne, P. & Messerschmidt, J. (2000). *Criminology* (3rd Ed.). Boulder, Colorado: Westview Press.

Block, P. (2002). Organization and Development. *Practicing OD 2002, 3*. Retrieved June 2006 from www.odnetwork.org

Bornstein, D. (2004). *How to change the world: Social entrepreneurs and the power of new ideas*. New York: Oxford University Press.

Burnett, P. H. (2004). *The true church: The path which led a Protestant lawyer to the Catholic church*. Antioch, California: Solas Press.

Catholic Bishops of the United States. (2002). *Responsibility, rehabilitation, and restoration: A Catholic perspective on crime and criminal justice*. Washington, D. C.: United States Catholic Conference.

Charles, Rodger S.J.. (1998). *Christian social witness and teaching: The Catholic tradition from Genesis to Centesimus Annus* (Vols. 1-2). Herefordshire, England: Gracewing Fowler Wright Books.

Charters, A. (Ed.). (1992). *The portable beat reader*. New York; Penguin Books.

Chautard, D. J., *The soul of the apostolate*. Trappist, Kentucky: Tan Books

Congregation for the Doctrine of the Faith. (1984). *Instruction on certain aspects of the "Theology of liberation"*. Retrieved March 14, 2007 from http://www.vatican.va/roman_curia/congregations/cfaith/documents/rc_con_cfaith_doc_19840806_theology-liberation_en.html

Congregation for the Doctrine of the Faith. (2006). *Notification on the Works of Father Jon Sobrino, SJ*. Retrieved March 14, 2007 from http://www.vatican.va/roman_curia/congregations/cfaith/documents/rc_con_cfaith_doc_20061126_notification-sobrino_en.html

Cummings, T. G. & Worley, C. G. (2005). *Organization development and change* (8th Ed.). Mason, Ohio: Thomson South Western.

Cummins, E. (1994). *The rise and fall of California's radical prison movement*. Stanford, California: Stanford University Press.

Douay-Rheims (2000) *New testament of our lord and savior Jesus Christ* (photographically reproduced from an unabridged edition of Haydock's Catholic Family Bible and

Commentary (1859). Monrovia, California: Catholic Treasures.

Ellul, J. (1970). *The meaning of the city*. Grand Rapids, Michigan: William B. Erdmans.

Ericson, E. E. Jr. & Mahoney, D. J. (eds.) (2006). *The Solzhenitsyn reader: New and essential writings 1947- 2005*. Wilmington, Delaware: ISI Books

Foley, L. & McCloskey, P. (2003). *Saint of the day: Lives lessons and feasts*. Cincinnati; St. Anthony Messenger Press.

Foucault, M. (1995) *Discipline & punish: The birth of the prison*. New York: Vintage Books.

Frazer, J. G. (1959). *The new golden bough*. (Gaster, T. H.Ed.). New York: Criterion Books.

Ginsburg, A. (1956) *Howl & other poems*. City Lights Books; San Francisco.

Gomez. J. H. Archbishop of San Antonio. (2007). *Homily: Annual Diocesan Red Mass*. Phoenix: St. Thomas More Society of Phoenix.

Gottschalk, M. (2006). *The prison and the gallows: The politics of mass incarceration in America*. New York: Cambridge University Press.

Hilderbrand, A. (2007, April). Truth or charity?. *Homiletic & Pastoral Review, 107*(7), 26-31.

Irwin, J. (1970). *The felon*. Englewood Cliffs, New Jersey: Prentice-Hall.

Hendershott, A. (2002). *The politics of deviance*. San Francisco: Encounter Books.

Holy See. (1997) *Catechism of the Catholic Church* (2nd Ed.) Rome: Libreria Editrice Vaticana.

Johnson, K. (2007, August 28) Criminals target each other, trend shows. *USA Today.* Retrieved August 31, 2007 from http://www.usatoday.com/news/nation/20 07- 08-31-criminal-target_N.htm?csp=34

Jurgens, W. A. (1970). *The faith of the early fathers: A source-book of theological and historical passages from the Christian writings of the Pre-Nicene and Nicene eras.* (Vols. 1-3). Collegeville, Minnesota: Liturgical Press.

Kennedy, S. (1997). (Ed.) *Spiritual journeys: An anthology of writings by people living and working with those on the margins.* Dublin, Ireland: Veritas.

Kennedy, S. S. & Bielfeld, W. (2006). *Charitable choice at work: Evaluating faith-based job programs in the States.* Washington D. C.: Georgetown University Press.

Kowalska, St. M. F., (2007). *Diary of Saint Maria Faustina Kowalska: Divine mercy in my soul.* (3rd ed. Revised). Stockbridge, Massachusetts: Marian Press.

Lawrence, T. E. (2000). *Seven pillars of wisdom: A triumph.* London: The Folio Society.

Lubac, H. D. (1982). *The motherhood of the church.* San Francisco, Ignatius Press.

Lukenbill, D. H. (2006). *The criminal's search for God: Criminal transformation, Catholic social teaching, deep knowledge leadership, and communal reentry.* (E-Book, 2nd ed.) Sacramento, CA: Chulu Press, Lampstand Foundation.

Mansfield, H. C. & Winthrop, D. (2000). *Alexis de Tocqueville (1835): Democracy in America*. Chicago: University of Chicago Press.

Maritain, J. (2001). *Natural law: Reflections on theory and practice*. South Bend, Indiana: St. Augustine's Press.

Maritain, J. & R. (1960). *Liturgy and contemplation*. London: Geoffrey Chapman.

Marks, F. W. (2007, July). John the Clarifier. *Homiletic & Pastoral Review, 108*(10), 10-17.

Merkle, J. A. (2004). *From the heart of the church: The Catholic social tradition*. Collegeville, Minnesota: Liturgical Press.

Miller, M. M. (2007). Women and the Catholic Priesthood. *First Things*. Retrieved September 26, 2007, from http://www.firstthings.com/onthesquare/?p=857

Morris, N. & Rothman, D. (1995). *The Oxford history of the prison: The practice of punishment in Western society*. New York: Oxford University Press.

Mumford, L. (1964). *The myth of the machine: The pentagon of power*. New York: Harcourt Brace Jovanovich.

Murray, C. (2000). *The Underclass Revisited*. AEI Online. Retrieved May 10, 2007 from http://www.aei.org/publications/pubID.14891/pub_detail.asp

Natapoff, A. (2004, December). Speechless: The silencing of criminal defendants [Electronic version]. *New York University Law Review, 80*(5), 1449-1504.

Navarre University (1999): *The Navarre Bible: The Pentateuch, commentary by members of the faculty of theology of the University of Navarre*. Princeton,NJ: Scepter Publishers.

Nonprofit Almanac (2007). *The nonprofit sector in brief.* Retrieved May 2007 from http://www.urban.org/UploadedPDF/31137 3_nonprofit_sector.pdf

Olasky, M. (2000). *Compassionate conservatism: What it is, what it does, and how it can transform America.* New York: The Free Press.

O'Neill, M. (2002). *Nonprofit nation: A new look at the third America.* San Francisco: Jossey-Bass.

Pontifical Council for Justice and Peace. (2004). *Compendium of the social doctrine of the church.* Vatican City: Libreria Editrice Vaticana.

Pope Benedict XVI. (2005). *Deus Caritas Est.* Retrieved October 11, 2007 from http://www.vatican.va/holy_father/benedic t_xvi/encyclicals/documents/hf_ben-xvi_enc_20051225_deus-caritas-est_en.html

Pope Benedict XVI. (2006, June 29). Capella Papale on the Solemnity of Peter and Paul, retrieved July 14, 2007 from www.vatican.va./holy_father/benedict_xvi/ homilies/2006/documents/hf_ben-xvi_hom_20060629_sts-peter-paul_en.html

Pope Benedict XVI. (2007, May 13). Pope's Address

to"Fazenda da Esperança" *"You Must Be Ambassadors of Hope"* Given at Guaratingueta, Brazil, May 13, 2007, Retrieved May 14 2007 from www.zenit.org .

Pope Benedict XVI. (2007). *Jesus of Nazareth: From the baptism in the Jordon to the Transfiguration.* New York: Doubleday.

Pope John Paul II. (1984) *Salvici Doloris:* Apostolic Letter, Retrieved April 27, 2007 from http://www.vatican.va/holy_father/john_p aul_ii/apost_letters/documents/hf_jp-ii_apl_11021984_salvifici-doloris_en.html

Pope John Paul II. (2000). Jubilee in Prisons: Message, Sunday July 9, 2000. Retrieved June 28, 2007 from http://www.vatican.va/jubilee_2000/jubile vents/events_jubil-prisoners_en.htm

Pope John Paul II. (2000). Jubilee in Prisons: Homily, Sunday July 9, 2000. Retrieved June 28, 2007 from http://www.vatican.va/jubilee_2000/jubile vents/events_jubil-prisoners_en.htm

Pope John Paul II. (2000). Jubilee in Prisons: Angelus, Sunday July 9, 2000. Retrieved June 28, 2007 from http://www.vatican.va/jubilee_2000/jubilc vents/events_jubil-prisoners_en.htm

Pope Gregory XVI. (1839). *In Supremo Apostolatus*: Apostolic Letter. Retrieved February 16, 2007 from www.ewtn.com/library/PAPALDOC/G16SU P.HTM .

Puhl, L. J. *SJ*. (1951). *The spiritual exercises of St.*

Ignatius. Chicago: Loyola Press.

Rimbaud, A. (1991). *A season in hell* and *Illuminations*. Brockport, New York: BOA Editions, Ltd.

Ross, J. I. & Richards, S. C. (2003). *Convict criminology*. Belmont, California: Thomson Wadsworth.

Samara, T. (n.d.). *Prisons, punishments, and profiteers*. Retrieved May 14, 2007 from http://louisville.edu/journal/workplace/issue6/samara.html

Schein, E. H. (1997). *Organizational culture and leadership* (2nd ed.). San Francisco: Jossey-Bass

Schindler, D. L.. (2006). Charity, Justice, and the Church's activity in the world, *Communio: International Catholic Review, 32*, 346-367

Shattuck, R. (1996). *Forbidden knowledge: From Prometheus to pornography*. New York: St. Martin's Press.

Skotnicki, A. (2000). *Religion and the development of the American penal system*. Lanham, Maryland: University Press of America.

Skotnicki, A. (2002, Winter/Spring). The U. S. Catholic bishops on crime and criminal justice. *Josephinum Journal of Theology, 9*(1) 146-157.

Skotnicki, A. (2004, December). Foundations once destroyed: The Catholic church and criminal justice. *Theological Studies, 65*(4) 792-816.

Skotnicki, A. (2006, January). God's prisoners: Penal confinement and the creation of Purgatory. *Modern Theology, 22*(1) 85-110.

Slevin, P., (2007, February 25). Ban on prison religious program challenged: U. S. Judge ruled evangelical rehabilitation effort in Iowa is unconstitutional, *Washington Post,* p.A-13

St. John of the Cross, (1991). *The collected works of St. John of the Cross* (K. Kavanaugh & O. Rodriguez, Trans.) Washington, D. C.. ICS Publications.

St. Thomas Aquinas. (1920). Summa Theologica, Retrieved March 7, 2008 from http://www.newadvent.org/summa/3025.htm

Tanguerey, A. (2000). *The spiritual life: A treatise on ascetical and mystical theology.* Rockford, Illinois: Tan Books and Publishers, Inc.

Taylor, M. L. (2001). *The executed God: The way of the cross in lockdown America.* Minneapolis: Fortress Press.

Travis, J. (2005). *But they all come back: Facing the challenges of prisoner reentry.* Washington D.C.: Urban Institute Press.

University of Navarre. (1988). *The Navarre Bible.* Dublin, Ireland: Four Courts Press.

U.S. Bishops. (2006). *Compendium: Catechism of the Catholic Church.* Washington, D.C. United States Conference of Catholic Bishops.

Vatican, *Catechism of the Catholic Church*: Retrieved September 24, 2007 from http://www.vatican.va/archive/ENG0015/_P7Z.HTM

Vatican. (2007). Congregation for the Doctrine of

the Faith. *Certain Aspects of Church Doctrine*. Retrieved July 26, 2007 from http://www.vatican.va/roman_curia/congregations/cfaith/documents/rc_con_cfaith_doc_20070629_res_ponsa quaestiones_en.html

Vieraitis, L. M., Kovandzic, T. V., & Marvell, T. B. (2007). The criminogenic effects of imprisonment: Evidence from state panel data, 1974-2002. *Criminology & Public Policy*.6, 589-622.

Washington State Institute of Public Policy. (2006, January). *Evidence-based corrections programs: What works and what does not.*

Whitehead, K. D. (2000). *One, holy, Catholic, and apostolic: The early Church was the Catholic Church*. San Francisco: Ignatius.

Wilson, J. Q. (1983). *Thinking about crime*. (Revised ed.). New York: Vintage Books.

Wilson, J. Q. (1993). *The moral sense*. New York: The Free Press

About the Author

David H. Lukenbill is a former criminal—
thief and robber—who has transformed his
life through education; an Associate of Arts
degree in Administration of Justice from
Sacramento City College, a Bachelor of
Science degree in Organizational Behavior
from the University of San Francisco, and a
Master of Public Administration degree
from the University of San Francisco;
several years developing, managing, and
consulting with criminal transformative
organizations, and a conversion to
Catholicism.

He is married to his wife of 25 years and
they have one child. They live by the
American River in California with two cats,
and all the wild critters they can feed.

Contact information at the Lampstand
Foundation website
www.lampstandfoundation.org

Prayer to St. Michael for Protection of The Catholic Church and Her Members

✠ Glorious St. Michael, Guardian and Defender of the Church of Jesus Christ, come to the assistance of the Church, against which the powers of Hell are unchained. Guard with thy special care her august visible head, and obtain for him and for us that the hour of triumph may speedily arrive.

✠ Glorious Archangel St. Michael, watch over us during life, defend us against the assaults of the demon, assist us especially at the hour of death, obtain for us a favorable judgment and the happiness of beholding God face to face for endless ages. Amen.

www.ingramcontent.com/pod-product-compliance
Lightning Source LLC
LaVergne TN
LVHW021456080426
835509LV00018B/2311